POStROaD

Post Road publishes twice yearly and accepts unsolicited poetry, fiction, and nonfiction submissions. Complete submission guidelines are available at www.postroadmag.com.

Subscriptions: Individuals, $18/year; Institutions, $34/year; outside the U.S. please add $6/year for postage.

Post Road is a nonprofit 501(c)(3) corporation published by Post Road Magazine, Inc. in partnership with the Boston College Department of English. All donations are tax-deductible.

Distributed by:

Ingram Periodicals, Inc., LaVergne, TN

Printed by:

BookMasters, Mansfield, OH

Post Road was founded in New York City in 1999 by Jaime Clarke and David Ryan with the following core editors: Rebecca Boyd, Susan Breen, Hillary Chute, Mark Conway, Pete Hausler, Kristina Lucenko (1999-2003), Anne McCarty and Michael Rosovsky.

Editors Emeritus include Sean Burke (1999-2001), Jaime Clarke (1999-2008), Mary Cotton, as Publisher and Managing Editor (2004-2008), Erin Falkevitz (2005-2006), Alden Jones (2002-2005), Fiona Maazel (2001-2002), Marcus McGraw (2003-2004), Catherine Parnell, as Managing Editor (2003), Samantha Pitchel (2006-2008), and Ricco Villanueva Siasoco, as Managing Editor (2009-2010).

Cover Art:
Lisa Beck, "Hidden Place", 2007
oil paint on canvas, 54x50"
image courtesy of the Artist and Feature Inc.

ISBN: 978-0-9849463-1-0

POStrOaD

Publisher
Post Road Magazine, Inc.
in partnership with the
Boston College Department
of English

Art Editor
Susan Breen

Criticism Editor
Hillary Chute

Fiction Editors
Rebecca Boyd
Mary Cotton
Michael Rosovsky
David Ryan

Guest Editor
Andrew Sofer

Nonfiction Editors
Josephine Bergin
Pete Hausler
Oona Patrick

Poetry Editors
Mark Conway
Anne McCarty
Nicolette Nicola
Jeffrey Shotts
Lissa Warren

Recommendations Editors
Tim Huggins
Nelly Reifler
Devon Sprague

Theatre Editor
David Ryan

Layout and Design
Josephine Bergin

Web Designer
David Ryan

Managing Editor
Christopher Boucher

Assistant Managing Editors
Sarah Berry
Elizabeth Bologna

Copyeditor
Valerie Duff-Strautmann

Interns
Laura Chilcoat
Katherine Fuccillo
Kate Iannarone
Michael Kadow
Catherine LeClair
Francesca McCaffrey
Jennifer O'Brien
Marissa Thornton

Readers
Jen Bergmark
Trey Brewer
Laura Chilcoat
Emily Copeland
Deirdre Costello
Kelly Cupo
Luke Dietrich
Julie Ertl
Catherine Gellene
Sara Gervais
Hannah Pfeifle Harlow
Kate Iannarone
Michael Kadow
Meghan Keefe
Katherine Kim
Jessa Kirk
Katie Kollef
Erica Plouffe Lazure
Ana Lopez
Stephen Lovely
Emily McLaughlin
James Melia
Amy Mikels
Tamzin Mitchell
Ashley Newsome
Brooke Olaussen
Carolyn Ownbey
Danica Pantic
Geoff Pierret
Colette Sartor
Andrew Schofield
Kate Shannon
Laura Smith
Chris Staudinger
Kate Sticca
Cam Terwilliger
Andrea Ruggirello
Dagmar Van Engen
Cedar Warman

Table of Contents

Theatre

Recommendations

Guest Folio

Contributor Notes

Lisa Abend is the author of *The Sorcerer's Apprentices: A Season in the Kitchen of Ferran Adria's elBulli*. Based in Madrid, she is the Spain correspondent for *Time* magazine, and she contributes frequently to the *New York Times, Bon Appetit, The Atlantic, AFAR*, and *Food and Wine*.

Christian Barter's first book, *The Singers I Prefer*, was a finalist for the Lenore Marshall Prize and his second book will be forthcoming in 2012 from BkMk Press. In '08-'09 he was a Hodder Fellow in poetry at Princeton. He is a trail crew supervisor at Acadia National Park and an editor for *The Beloit Poetry Journal*.

Kaveh Bassiri is the co-founder of Triptych Readings and the Literary Arts Director of the Persian Art Festival in New York City. He was the recipient of the 2010 Witter Bynner Translation Residency and the 2011 Walton Translation Fellowship. His poetry won the *Bellingham Review*'s 49th Parallel Award and was recently published in *Virginia Quarterly Review, Drunken Boat*, and *Mississippi Review*.

Born in 1982, **Stefan Merrill Block** grew up in Texas. His first novel, *The Story of Forgetting*, won Best First Fiction at the Rome International Festival of Literature, the 2008 Merck Serono Literature Prize, and the 2009 Fiction Award from The Writers' League of Texas. *The Story of Forgetting* was also a finalist for the debut fiction awards from IndieBound, Salon du Livre, and The Center for Fiction. His second novel, *The Storm at the Door*, was released in the summer of 2011. He lives in Brooklyn.

James Boice was born in 1982 in Salinas, California and grew up in northern Virginia. He is the author of the critically acclaimed novels *The Good and the Ghastly, NoVA*, and *MVP*. His work has appeared in *Esquire, McSweeney's, Fiction, Salt Hill*, and other publications. He dropped out of college after three weeks to be a writer. He lives in New York and writes about pathological people.

Amy Boutell is a graduate of Barnard College and holds an MFA from the University of Texas, where she was a James A. Michener Fellow. Her short stories have been published in *New Letters, Nimrod*, and *Other Voices*, and she has been a finalist for the Katherine Anne Porter Prize for Fiction, the Tobias Wolff Award for Fiction, and the William Faulkner Short Story Competition. She has been awarded scholarships and fellowships by the Norman Mailer Writers Colony, the Ragdale Foundation, and Summer Literary Seminars. She is currently revising her first novel, which is set in the world of vintage fashion in Los Angeles and was a runner-up for the 2011 Pirate's Alley/Faulkner Society Novel-in-Progress Competition. She lives in Santa Barbara and works as an instructor at UCSB's Writing Lab.

Nora Cameron is a senior in high school. She lives in Cambridge, MA. This is her first published story.

Maggie Dietz is the author of *Perennial Fall* (University of Chicago Press, 2006). The former director of the Favorite Poem Project, she teaches at the University of Massachusetts Lowell.

Rhina P. Espaillat has published poems, essays, short stories, and translations in numerous magazines and over fifty anthologies, in both English and her native

Spanish, as well as three chapbooks and eight full-length books, including three in bilingual format. Her most recent are a poetry collection in English, *Her Place in These Designs* (Truman State University Press, Kirksville, 2008), and a bilingual collection of her short stories, *El olor de la memoria/The Scent of Memory* (Ediciones CEDIBIL, Santo Domingo, D. R., 2007). Her honors include the Wilbur Award, the T. S. Eliot Prize in Poetry, the Robert Frost "Tree at My Window" Award for Translation, the May Sarton Award, a Lifetime Achievement in the Arts Award from Salem State College, and several prizes from the Dominican Republic's Ministry of Culture.

Atar Hadari was born in Israel, raised in England, and trained as an actor and writer at the University of East Anglia before winning a scholarship to study poetry and playwrighting with Derek Walcott at Boston University. His plays have won awards from the BBC, Arts Council of England, National Foundation of Jewish Culture (New York), European Association of Jewish Culture (Brussels) and the Royal Shakespeare Company, where he was Young Writer in Residence. Plays have been staged at the Finborough Theatre, Wimbledon Studio Theatre, Chichester Festival Theatre, the Mark Taper Forum (where he was a Mentor Playwright), Nat Horne Studio Theatre (New York) and Valdez, Alaska. His *Songs from Bialik: Selected Poems of H. N. Bialik* (Syracuse University Press) was a finalist for the American Literary Translators' Association Award, and his poems have won the Daniel Varoujan award from New England Poetry Club, the Petra Kenney award, a Paumanok poetry award and many other prizes.

Jim Hett lives in Connecticut. He has exhibited his work at the Aldrich Contemporary Art Museum, the Katonah Museum of Art, the New York Public Library, New York University and the University of Connecticut.

Owen Hill is the author of several small poetry collections, a book of short stories, and two mystery novels, *The Chandler Apartments* and *The Incredible Double*. A pamphlet, *Union Steward*, is just out from Decentralized Publications. He works as a buyer and events coordinator at Moe's Books in Berkeley.

Jenn Hollmeyer is a founding editor of *Fifth Wednesday Journal* and received her MFA from the Bennington Writing Seminars. Her stories, essays, and poems have appeared in *Meridian, Etching, Quality Fiction, A Prairie Journal* and other journals. Jenn also paints architectural portraits and works as a marketing copywriter. She lives near Chicago.

Caitlin Horrocks is author of the story collection *This Is Not Your City*. Her stories appear in *The Best American Short Stories 2011, The PEN/ O. Henry Prize Stories 2009, The Pushcart Prize XXXV, The Paris Review*, and elsewhere. She lives in Grand Rapids, Michigan and teaches at Grand Valley State University.

Sean Keck is in the English PhD program at Brown University, where he examines 19th-and-20th century American literature through the lens of media studies. His poetry has appeared in *Concho River Review, Eclipse*, and Poetry Society of America-sponsored posters on the St. Louis Metro. He has lived in New Jersey, Missouri (twice), Oregon (twice), Massachusetts, and (currently) Rhode Island.

Michael Kimball is the author of three novels, including *Dear Everybody* (which *The Believer* calls "a curatorial masterpiece") and, most recently, *Us* (which was named to *Oprah's* Reading List). His work has been on NPR's *All Things Considered* and in *Vice*, as well as *The Guardian, Bomb*, and *New York Tyrant*, and has been translated into a dozen languages. He is also responsible for *Michael Kimball Writes Your Life Story* (on a postcard). His new novel, *Big Ray*, will be published by Bloomsbury in Fall 2012.

Dave King's debut novel, *The Ha-Ha*, was named one of the best books of 2005 by the *Washington Post* and other venues and earned him the 2006 John Guare Writers Fund Rome Prize Fellowship from the American Academy of Arts and Letters. King's poems and essays have appeared in *The Paris Review, The Village Voice, Ninth Letter, Big City Lit*, and the Italian literary journal *Nuovi Argomenti*. He divides his time between Brooklyn and the Hudson Valley of New York. A new novel, tentatively entitled *The Beast and Beauty*, is forthcoming.

Len Krisak's latest books are translations of *Virgil's Eclogues* and *The Complete Odes of Horace*. He has work in *AGNI, The Hudson Review, The Sewanee Review*, and *London Magazine*, and is a four-time champion on Jeopardy!

Anna Leahy's *Constituents of Matter* won the Wick Poetry Prize, and her poems and prose appear regularly in literary journals such as *Crab Orchard Review, Cream City Review, The Journal, The Southern Review*, and others. She edited *Power and Identity in the Creative Writing Classroom* (Multilingual Matters). She teaches in the MFA and BFA programs at Chapman University, where she directs Tabula Poetica and its annual reading series. For more info: www.amleahy.com.

Holly LeCraw is the author of *The Swimming Pool*, a Kirkus 2010 Top Debut, which was recently released in paperback. Her story "August," which appeared in *Post Road 8*, was nominated for a Pushcart Prize. She lives outside Boston with her family, where she is at work on her next novel.

Jim Lewis is the author of three novels–most recently, *The King is Dead*—and numerous essays on visual art.

Cynthia Northcutt Malone is a professor of English at the College of Saint Benedict and Saint John's University. Her current research projects focus on Laurence Sterne, Charles Dickens, and the evolution of the book.

Sally Wen Mao is an 826 Valencia Young Author's Scholar and a Kundiman fellow. Her work can be found published or forthcoming in *Fourteen Hills, Gulf Coast, Hayden's Ferry Review, Sycamore Review*, and *West Branch*, among others. Born in Wuhan, China, she has lived in Boston, the Bay Area, Pittsburgh, Amsterdam, and most recently Ithaca, where she is an MFA candidate at Cornell University.

Delaney Nolan's fiction has appeared or is forthcoming in *Grist, Arts & Letters PRIME, Contrary, Gargoyle*, online at *Monkeybicycle*, and elsewhere. She is twenty-two, she lives in New Orleans, her neighbor keeps a fake leg in her house but she has both her legs, and yesterday she saw an alligator.

Catherine Parnell teaches writing and literature at Suffolk University, as well as the occasional seminar at Grub Street in Boston. She's the fiction editor for *Salamander*, an associate editor for *Consequence Magazine*, and an editor for Anomalous Press. Her recent and forthcoming publications include stories and reviews in *The Baltimore Review, Slush Pile, roger, Diverse Voices Quarterly*,

Dos Passos Review, *Painted Bride Quarterly*, *Stone's Throw Magazine*, and *Another Book*, as well as various newspapers and newsletters. Her nonfiction chapbook, *The Kingdom of His Will*, was published in 2007 by Arrowsmith Press.

After riding through the Cote d'Azur Mountains and surviving a swarm of angry bees, **D. Gatling Price** managed to complete his first Ironman Triathlon in Nice, France. He is a graduate of the University of Southern California Creative Writing Program and has previously published in *Post Road* as well as the *New Orleans Review*.

Jane Roper is the author of a novel, *Eden Lake*, and a memoir, *Double Time*, forthcoming from St. Martin's Press. Her writing has appeared in *Poets & Writers*, *Salon*, *The Rumpus*, Babble.com and elsewhere. She lives outside of Boston with her husband and twin daughters. Her website is www.janeroper.com.

Joshua Ruffin received his MFA from Georgia College & State University, where he now teaches. He has also held jobs as a bartender, freelance journalist, peach picker, trail crew worker, and very unintimidating bouncer. His poetry has appeared or is forthcoming in *Eclipse*, *The Southeast Review*, *The Pinch*, *491 Magazine*, and *Poetry South*.

Peter Schireson is a Zen Buddhist priest living and writing in the foothills of the Sierras in California. His work has appeared in *Grey Sparrow Journal*, *Midwest Literary Magazine*, *Annalemma*, *Flashquake*, and *poetrysuperhighway*, among others.

Skye Shirley graduated in 2010 from Boston College with a major in English Literature and Creative Writing. Skye has most recently been a featured reader at the Brookline Poetry Series and the Calliope Poetry Series. Upon the completion of her first poetry manuscript, *The Good Women*, Skye received the Dever Fellowship for Creative Writing. Her poems have been awarded the McCarthy Prize, Kelleher Poetry Prize, and the Gary Fincke Poetry Prize. Her work has been published by numerous journals, including *The Sow's Ear Poetry Review*, *Best Undergraduate Writing of 2009*, and *Susquehanna Review*.

Curtis Smith's most recent books are *Bad Monkey* (stories, Press 53), *Truth or Something Like It* (novel, Casperian Books), and *Witness* (essays, Sunnyoutside Press).

Michael Sowder's poetry collection, *The Empty Boat*, won the 2004 T.S. Eliot Award; *A Calendar of Crows* won the New Michigan Press Award; and his study of Walt Whitman, *Whitman's Ecstatic Union*, was published by Routledge Press. *House Under the Moon*, a collection of poems about fatherhood and the bhakti tradition of Kabir, is forthcoming next year. He is currently at work on a spiritual memoir, and his essays about Buddhism and poetry appear in the Buddhist magazine *Shambhala Sun*. He teaches at Utah State University in Logan, Utah, where he lives with his wife and two sons.

Amanda Stern is the author of the novel *The Long Haul*. She's been published in *The New York Times*, *The New York Times Magazine*, *The Believer*, *FiveChapters*, *St. Ann's Review* and others. In 2003, she founded The Happy Ending Music and Reading Series, which she runs out of Joe's Pub, part of the Public Theater.

Daniel Tobin is the author of five books of poems, most recently *Belated Heavens* (Four Way Books), which won the Massachusetts Book Award in Poetry. His book of essays, *Awake in America*, is newly out from Notre Dame. His awards include fellowships from the National Endowment for the Arts and the John Simon Guggenheim Foundation. He is currently interim Dean of the School of the Arts at Emerson College.

Jennifer Tonge's poetry has appeared most recently in *Copper Nickel*. She lives in Salt Lake City.

Addie Tsai received her MFA in Poetry from Warren Wilson College. Her work has been published in *NOON: A Journal of the Short Poem*, *American Letters & Commentary*, *Forklift, Ohio*, *Caketrain*, and *Yellow as Turmeric, Fragrant as Cloves: A Contemporary Anthology of Asian American Women's Poetry*, among others. Her work has been most recently published in the anthology *Collective Brightness: LGBTIQ Poets on Faith, Religion & Spirituality* and her nonfiction is forthcoming from Pebble Lake Review. Her manuscript *and in its place—* was semi-finalist in *Tupelo Press's* 2009 *Dorset Prize* and a finalist in *Four Way Books'* 2011 *Larry Levis Prize*. She was co-conceiver of Dominic Walsh Dance Theater's production *Victor Frankenstein*, and she exhibited a series of photographic collage work, *the body as landscape: the body as terror: the body as ecstasy* in collaboration with Traci Matlock. Addie currently teaches Literature and Composition at Houston Community College, where she runs a nationally-known reading series.

Alissa Tsukakoshi is a recipient of a Hopwood Award in short fiction. She received her MA in creative writing from Boston University.

Melanie Unruh received her MFA in creative writing from the University of New Mexico. Her work has appeared in *New Ohio Review* and *Pear Noir!*, and is forthcoming from *Echo Ink Review*. She's currently finishing her first novel, *At the Rim of Vision*.

Rimas Uzgiris' poetry has been published in *Bridges*, *322 Review*, *Lituanus*, *Prime Number Magazine*, *The Poetry Porch*, and is forthcoming in *Quiddity*. His translations have appeared in *The Massachusetts Review*, *Spork Press*, and are forthcoming in *Modern Poetry in Translation*, *Hayden's Ferry Review*, *Lituanus*, and *Two Lines Online*. Uzgiris received his MFA in creative writing from Rutgers-Newark University, where he studied poetry with Rigoberto Gonzalez and Rachel Hadas. He also holds a PhD in philosophy from the University of Wisconsin-Madison. His philosophical monograph, *Desire, Meaning, and Virtue: The Socratic Account of Poetry*, was published in 2009.

Adam Vines received his MFA from the University of Florida. He is an assistant professor of English at the University of Alabama at Birmingham, where he edits *Birmingham Poetry Review* and serves as faculty advisor for the UAB Fishing Team. His poems have appeared in *North American Review*, *32 Poems*, *The Cincinnati Review*, *Third Coast*, *Barrow Street*, *The Literary Review*, *Greensboro Review*, *New Orleans Review*, among others. The University of Arkansas Press will publish his first collection, *The Coal Life*, in 2012. During the summers, he is on staff at the Sewanee Writers' Conference.

Zachary Watterson's essays, articles, and stories appear in *The Massachusetts Review*, *The Stranger*, *Sendero*, *Struggle*, *Salt River Review*, and *River Styx*, among many other publications. Originally from New York City, Zachary played collegiate basketball in Colorado and South Africa. A Pushcart Prize nominee and recipient of multiple scholarships to the Bread Loaf Writers' Conference, he received a 2010 fellowship from the Jentel Arts Foundation, was a semifinalist for a 2011 fellowship from the Fine Arts Work Center in Provincetown, and is the recipient of a 2011 grant from the Elizabeth George Foundation.

Writers and Critics at the Dinner Table: TRISTRAM SHANDY as Conversational Model

Cynthia Northcutt Malone

There is nothing so foolish, when you are at the expence of making an entertainment of this kind, as to order things so badly, as to let your criticks and gentry of refined taste run it down: Nor is there any thing so likely to make them do it, as that of leaving them out of the party, or, what is full as offensive, of bestowing your attention upon the rest of your guests in so particular a way, as if there was no such thing as a critick (by occupation) at table.

—I guard against both; for, in the first place, I have left half a dozen places purposely open for them;—and, in the next place, I pay them all court,—

—Laurence Sterne, *Tristram Shandy* (II.ii.60)

Digital media make possible the blending, fusing, even violent yoking of forms and genres: animated typography with audio; virtual historical sites with documents and video. Some mixtures yield glorious results; some fizzle; some reek. Oddly, two related textual forms have so far largely resisted the forces of mashup. Literary works and critical responses— reviews, scholarly essays, blog postings, and the like—typically inhabit separate discursive spaces. A few exceptions, especially critical editions and casebooks, do bind together literary works and critical essays. Yet, on the whole, critical and literary works resist fusion.

Criticism attracts criticism; scholarly studies accrue citations as they roll along. (That scholarly articles often cite earlier articles in order to wad them up and toss them in the bin, clearing space for the work at hand—never mind that just now.) And critical essays do quote bits of the texts they examine. As for literary works, almost anything sticks like a burr in their shaggy coats, any text from *Paradise Lost* to a chewing-gum jingle. Contemporary experimental writing invites collaboration of many kinds, yet rarely, even now, does a writer allow critical work to lodge in a literary text.

To borrow Sterne's metaphor, writers and criticks [see above] usually take their meals in separate dining rooms. The publisher distributes a work; the reviewer, scholar, or citizen blogger publishes a response. Occasionally a writer feels moved to respond to the criticism and sends a letter to an editor, or an interviewer asks the writer about specific matters in a critical response. These exchanges only illuminate the conventional separation between the literary work and the critical response, as an exchange of letters highlights the fact of separate postal addresses. How odd, how quaint that separation seems in a digital environment of crossovers.

Laurence Sterne bridged the separation 250 years ago, with Volume III of *Tristram Shandy*. As the epigraph demonstrates, *Tristram Shandy* first sets places for the criticks in Volume I, published in 1760; Tristram then mocks, scolds, beefs about, and quarrels with them in Volume III, published a year later. By the time Sterne composed Volume III, Volumes I and II had proven a sensation. Moreover, Sterne's publication of *The Sermons of Mr. Yorick* had provoked great ire. When writing Volume III, then, Sterne had his pick of critics to seat at his dinner table as guests or targets. One example illustrates the point: the *Monthly Review* had featured a review of Volumes I and II in the form of a fictional dialogue between Sir John and Sir Peter, a traveller just returned to England. Sir Peter asks about recent developments in his home country, and Sir John winds up a scathing description of *Tristram Shandy* with this summary: "In few words, Sir, and without a figure, *Tristram Shandy* is an obscene novel, the reverend author is a prebend of the church of England; and both are at present in the highest estimation" (qtd. in Howes 96). Sterne deploys Tristram to answer this review. Comparing the body and mind to a jerkin and its lining, Tristram complains that "never poor jerkin has been tickled off, at such a rate as it has been these last nine months together": "—You Messrs. the monthly Reviewers!—how could you cut and slash my jerkin as you did?—how did you know, but you would cut my lining too?" (III.iv.115).

It was the serial publication of *Tristram Shandy*, of course, that gave Sterne the opportunity to answer the reviewers of earlier volumes. In fact, serial publication created the possibility not only for responses to reviewers, but also for topical commentary on and references to public events. In *Sterne, the Moderns, and the Novel*, Thomas Keymer notes that Volume IX of the novel "jestingly" alludes "to unrelated developments in the external world . . . by playing on the fact that the commoner to whom volume 1 is dedicated [William Pitt] has in the interim become a peer" (103). While Sterne's model may have tempted other writers of serial fiction to tease or torment their critics, those other writers generally chose to bar critics from the dining rooms of their novels. Serial publication simultaneously made possible a response to critics and fixed writers' minds wholly on the next developments of their own narratives. By the Victorian period, when serial publication in periodicals became common, publishers' deadlines drove writers so relentlessly that many had to write flat-out to complete an installment. Pausing in this sprint to engage in a playful exchange with reviewers must have been the farthest thing from their minds.

Thanks to the digital storage of texts, contemporary writers could easily graft the words of a critic or reviewer into a literary work. The digital era simplifies the creation of hybrid forms: just as mixing musical tracks once required great labor and technical skill, so splicing criticism into a literary work once required tedious resetting of the text. Now, however, a writer could invite critics to enter one version of his or her literary text and exile the critics from another, shaping multiple versions of the "same" work. Writers and critics could work collaboratively, creating hybrid forms that emphasize the dialogue between writer and reader.

Certainly the familiar, separate forms of "creative" and "critical" or "scholarly" writing will and should persist, since these different forms of work grant considerable pleasure and insight. They persist because writers and readers value the experiences of entering an imagined world and residing there until the last speck of punctuation, or of following a perceptive and well-informed extended argument. We need not choose between those inherited forms and hybrid forms. Older forms will remain even as hybrid forms emerge alongside them.

If the writer were to invite the critic to dinner, what might the hybrid form look like? Let's take John Banville's 2010 novel, *The Infinities*. Set in a house called Arden, the novel features both mortals and gods. Lest we think that the gods have given up their Olympian mount for the damp and gloom of an Irish home, Hermes explains early in the novel that "the gods cannot but be everywhere"—not only in Arden, not only in "this rough world," but also in "an infinity of others just like it that we made and must keep ever vigilantly in our care" (14). As we begin reading the novel, its world appears to be the world that readers know (except, of course, for the gods lurking about). In the opening pages, natural laws operate as we'd expect: ill-fitting pajamas pinch, uneaten cereal congeals. Soon enough, though, the narrator makes an offhand allusion to history that arrests us in our tracks. Hermes refers to "Mary, Queen of Scots, great Gloriana" (36). Mary as Gloriana? Hasn't Hermes read Spenser? The passage goes on to recount Mary's "accession to the English throne after the beheading of her cousin, the upstart and treasonous Elizabeth Tudor" (36).

The contemporary world of the novel bristles with surprises, too: scientists have debunked "Wallace's theory of evolution" and string theory; they have successfully managed cold fusion; the country derives most of its energy from brine (82, 103, 93, 94). The world of the novel coincides nearly, but not entirely, with the world we know. Gradually we realize that the world from which Hermes recounts this story is not the world the reader inhabits but another, one of the "infinity of others" he alluded to in the early pages.

If he wished, Banville could extrapolate from the notion of infinite worlds: the thematics of infinite possibility *in* the novel might be turned to illustrate the infinite possibilities *of* the novel. Suppose, for example,

Banville were to create in addition to the published, printed 2010 novel another version, integrating into it the remarks of selected reviewers. For example, Banville might respond to Christopher Tayler's criticism of the narrator's style, which appeared in *The Guardian*: "Hermes, if he is Hermes, overwrites shamelessly. Banville has shown before that a heavy gloss of style doesn't have to rule out artistic restraint and some resemblance to a speaking voice, but, sad to say, he doesn't do so here." No one is likely to refute the point about overwriting, but Tayler links this observation about style with a crucial question about the narrator's identity: "Hermes, if he is Hermes." That qualifying conditional, "if he is," matters greatly, and it repays reflection.

At strategic points in *The Infinities*, wobbly pronouns blur distinctions between "narrator" and "character," and the ambiguous pronoun references raise questions about cause and effect, about perspectives and evidence, and about the workings-out that constitute the closure of the novel. If Banville chose to respond to Tayler in another version of his novel, what divine jujitsu Hermes might visit on Tayler. The charge of overwriting might prompt Banville to marble the narrative with new asides to the reader on the subject of style, moments of self-justification or self-mockery. Those revisions would result in a version that nearly coincides, but doesn't quite, with the 2010 novel. Any provocative observation about the novel—from a review, a scholarly essay, or a blog—could generate another of its infinite possibilities.

Jorge Luis Borges would surely smile upon this narrative experiment, but what good might it do for the world that writers and critics share? *Tristram Shandy* pictures the writer and reader—or the specialized reader, "the critic (by occupation)"—in conversation, and a livelier exchange offers several potential benefits. Anyone who has ever belonged to a book group or enrolled in a literature class has noticed that legions of readers half-perceive and half-create the works they read. To put the point another way, discussions reveal that many readers have in mind a work that nearly coincides, but doesn't quite, with the work on the page. A writer who invites a critic to the table would confront (with delight or chagrin) the phenomenon of infinite readings and misreadings. Conversation with the reader may yield nothing but a fuller awareness on each side of error and blindness—misleadings and misreadings the writer failed to anticipate, misreadings that the reader wandered into. But the digitally enabled extensions of a literary work might take forms that reach far beyond clarification: dialogue embedded in the text, generating new imaginative directions for a narrative, lyric, essay, or dramatic work; dialogue in the margins, supplementing the voice of the work with multiply voiced inquiry and commentary. Works like McKenzie Wark's *Gamer Theory* point the way. Working with the Institute for the Future of the Book, Wark published *Gamer Theory* online, along with a forum for comments and discussion. Readers' comments informed the revision, *Gamer Theory 2.0*; the print version, published in 2006 by Harvard University Press, contains selections from the discussion. The most innovative works might follow this model: born as openings for dialogue, recognizing from their inception the collaborative enterprise of writing and reading. Even in these works, of course, the writer could issue the invitations and operate the dining-room door; the writer could choose the number and names of those invited to dinner. What might happen around the table we can no more anticipate than we can predict what will happen at our own liveliest dinner parties.

> —Gentlemen, I kiss your hands,—I protest no company could give me half the pleasure,—by my soul I am glad to see you,— beg only you will make no strangers of yourselves, but sit down without any ceremony, and fall on heartily. (II.ii.60)

Gather interesting minds around the table: it's time for dinner. ঌ

Works Cited

Banville, John. *The Infinities*. New York: Knopf, 2010.

Howes, Alan B., ed. *Laurence Sterne: The Critical Heritage*. 1971. London and New York: Routledge, 1995.

Keymer, Thomas. *Sterne, the Moderns, and the Novel*. Oxford: Oxford UP, 2002.

Sterne, Laurence. *The Life and Opinions of Tristram Shandy, Gentleman*. Ed. Howard Anderson. 1760-1767. New York and London: Norton, 1980.

Tayler, Christopher. "*The Infinities* by John Banville." guardian.co.uk. *The Guardian*, 25 September 2009. Web. 22 February 2011.

We Shared a Duplex

Jenn Hollmeyer

Anna lived in the east half.

I lived in the west half.

At first I thought we would be friends.

I didn't have a cat at first.

Anna had a cat. She called it Storm.

When she called it, people across the neighborhood shut their windows and brought in their laundry.

I opened my windows and took out my laundry.

Sometimes it wasn't actual laundry. I hung junk mail and coupons and want ads, just to hear them beg in the breeze. Sometimes I hung a bra for effect.

Anna saw the effect.

You should get a cat, she said.

I unpinned the want ads and found kittens, flee to a good home.

Flee, it said.

I picked one out the same color as Storm.

I called it Hannah.

When I called it, Anna came to her window. ❧

How to Remember the Dead

Curtis Smith

A Saturday afternoon, and my seven-year-old is uncharacteristically quiet. He sits on the couch, his hands clasped. He says he is not sick, yet he doesn't want to go to the playground, doesn't want to throw the football or Frisbee, doesn't want to play a game or draw or build Legos. "No, thank you," he says when I offer to turn on the TV. "I just want some alone time."

Ten minutes later, I'm ready to engage him again. I will offer a trip to the local zoo. Or a hike to see if the falling leaves have exposed the nest of the bald eagle we've spotted along our trail. Perhaps just a trip to K-mart to ogle the toy-aisle goodies. I return to the living room to discover my son on my wife's lap. He's burrowed his face into her shoulder, his sobs muffled. She holds him close and whispers everything is all right.

My heart tightens. Our boy is not the crying type. He takes his lumps in hockey and karate without complaint. He doesn't whine about school or playground cliques. If we tell him a desired item is too expensive, he won't mention it again. I rub his heaving back. "What's wrong, bud?" I ask.

He holds out a hand and unclenches his fingers. In his palm, a silver half-dollar, Walking Liberty, the coin's relief worn smooth, tarnished brown in its nooks. For a moment, I'm perplexed. I turn it over once more before noting the date. 1936. The year my father was born.

My friend is dying. The disease has spread. Lungs, bones, bladder—little has been spared. He lies in the bed from which he will never rise, his bodily functions shunted to plastic bags. I pull up a chair. He remains lucid, and we talk as men often do—teasing, joking, remembering. We exchange stories of our children and the joy they've brought to our lives. His voice fades into a whisper. The hands that guided a kayak through white water and built a house in the woods struggle to unscrew his water bottle's cap. He asks if I would say a few words at his funeral. I tell him I'd be honored.

My son prefers documentaries to cartoons. War, science, nature—give him archival footage and a passionate narrator, and he will grow entranced, his toy of the moment abandoned by his side. He drinks in facts and repeats them later with eerie precision. He will tell you the different planes Manfred von Richthofen flew. He will relate the cautionary tale of Thomas Andrews and his unsinkable ocean liner. He will break down the wind speeds that separate an EF3 tornado from an EF4.

Tonight, it's Vesuvius and doomed Pompeii, and as it often happens,

I, too, become rapt by another mismatch of man's ambitions and nature's might. A suffocation of searing ash and gas. A burial beneath a pumice flow. A decay of flesh, skeletons sealed in ashy tombs. Years pass, the city forgotten, the millennia marked by man's ever-increasing skill at killing his brothers. Then discovery, bones at first, complete skeletons cowering against death's blind rush.

A new technique emerges, plaster injected into the hollowed spaces, the hardened product as detailed as a mold. Here are no longer skeletons; here are silent and tragic stories. The beggar and his sack of alms. The gladiators shackled in their cell. The mother huddled over her infant daughter.

A commercial breaks the spell. I consider the possible haunting of these images, and I switch to the hockey game, the only sport that interests my son. The game is exciting—a breakaway and an acrobatic save, a crashing along the boards, a melee at the net that ends with overmatched referees struggling to keep peace.

My son looks up to me. "Daddy, can we go back to Vesuvius?"

I park in front of my friend's house. I'm nervous today. His end is near; he has days, perhaps a week. His wife thanks me and shows me to his room. The hospice nurse has taped his morphine pump to his hand. He manages a smile and says he'd share the good stuff if he could.

We talk about the students we knew as children now grown with children of their own. When his mouth goes dry, he sips water, then asks if I'll hold the waste can while he weighs the necessity of vomiting. As I hold the can, I recall the hot summer day we tore shingles off his roof, the morning we spread the concrete foundation of his garage. I joke, reminding him we've had our share of barroom escapades, and this wouldn't be the first time I'd seen him retch.

The nausea passes, but it's not a good day. When the spasms come, each breath becomes a struggle. He sucks his chapped lips, presses the morphine pump. The pain is palpable, a dark energy that ebbs from his body. He grows tired. I stand, and with the perspective switch, I realize I will never see him again. I want to say goodbye, but I can't. We shake, a grasping of thin, taped fingers. "See you around, brother," I say.

He smiles. "Or maybe not."

My son and I arrive at the church to light a candle for my father's birthday, the second he will miss. The candle is my son's idea—he and my father shared a bond I couldn't have predicted. The hell-bent toddler calmed at his grandfather's side, fascinated by his visitor's cane and bald head. They shared odd silences—my father with his malfunctioning hearing aids, my son with his lack of understanding—each content to sit near the other, my son often mesmerized by the glide of his fingers over the old man's papery skin.

All is quiet inside the church. Despite my best intentions, we've missed my father's birthday, even his birthday week, done in by colds and hockey practices, by the Indian summer afternoons where a playground romp seemed the most responsible course of action. Today, the low autumn sun strikes the stained glass, the cavernous space awash in light. The candles are arranged on a rack off the altar. I give my son money to slide into the collection box. Whispering, I guide him through the process, my hands not far as he uses a wooden stick to transfer a flame to a candle's wick. The flame catches. The candle's frosted glass shimmers.

I'm leading us to a nearby pew when my son stops me. "The book, Daddy," he whispers.

Beside the candle rack, a journal rests atop a metal stand. I offer my son the pen resting in the pages' opened nook. "No, you," he says.

He wedges himself between me and the bookstand, the page just below his eye level. I jot the date, and after a moment: *For our father and grandfather. We miss you.*

I put down the pen, but my boy tugs my sleeve. "And for the people of Pompeii," he whispers. "I want to remember them, too."

I pick up the pen and add: *And a special thought for those who died at Pompeii.*

He smiles. "That's good, Daddy."

We settle into a pew. Above the altar hangs a giant plaster Christ on the cross, slumped shoulders and bony ribs, a crown of thorns for his head. The sculpture once terrified my son, and in his lifted gaze, a bit of that fear remains. I put my arm around his shoulders and study his prayer-clasped hands. My father was a complicated man, as stern and hard as he was loving. Through my son's eyes, I've been granted a new perspective, that rarest of gifts, and I join him in clasping my hands. Silence, but we're not alone. Nearby, a woman kneels, the beads of her rosary slipping between her fingers. In another pew, an old man, his face hidden in his hands.

I consider the suffering etched onto Christ's face. I think of the dead, and I think of the deeper level of death, the death born when all those I ever knew will be gone too, the earth populated by strangers. Later tonight, a priest will snuff our candle, and its dying whiff will rise to the high ceiling. There it will mingle with the smoke from other candles, each lit for a prayer or soul I will never know.

My boy stands. "Ready, Daddy?" he asks.

We head outside, squinting in the cold sun. He slips his hand in mine.

I receive the news that my friend has died on a Friday morning. I call in sick. I have no desire to spend the day in the building where we taught together for so many years. I'm writing in the dim morning light, the sun not yet above the trees, when I hear the slap of bare feet on the stairs.

"Daddy?" He halts on the last step and considers me through weary eyes. He pulls at the hem of his skull-and-cross-bone pajamas. "What're you doing here?"

"I'm going in a little later." I rub his head. It's my second lie of the day, but my guilt-sensitive heart is unbothered. "What do you want for breakfast?"

Together, he, my wife, and I enjoy an unhurried morning. We eat waffles and talk about Vesuvius. He picks up the half dollar from the end table. "Still thinking about Grandpa?" I ask.

"Some." He returns the coin to the table. "What made me sad was that I know I miss him, but sometimes I have trouble remembering him."

The bus comes, but instead of hustling out, we drive to school today. On the way, we talk about how my father would be proud of the young man his grandson has become. We recount the ways my boy made the old man laugh and the games the two of them liked to play. When we reach the school, our son is smiling. His pack slung over his shoulders, he approaches the entrance, a journey made with a friend he meets along the way. In a heartbeat, he disappears into the throng.

I wake early, my night beset by odd dreams. The service starts at 2:00, almost eight hours, a chunk of time that this morning seems suddenly vast. In my office, I sip coffee and revisit the words I'll offer at the funeral. Soon, the house stirs, the Saturday-morning chatter of my wife and son. I want to join them, but I need to finish my work. I cover my ears, a whispered reading that resonates in my head alone. I am not a poet, but this morning I feel the poet's burden of weighing each word before committing it to the final draft.

Kisses are exchanged before my wife and geared-up son leave for hockey practice, but even in our now-silent home, I find myself distracted, unfocused by the familiarity of these rooms. I don my hat and coat and head out for a walk. I pass backyard play sets, nod hello to a neighbor raking the season's last leaves. A bike rider zooms past. In the air, the scent of wood smoke. Later today I will rise into a pulpit and gaze upon scores of teary faces. I will stifle my emotions and share my thoughts on the gift of remembering the dead. A man's deeds must outlive his flesh, his acts of doing a brand of kinetic energy yet to be understood by physicists. Death is one's final ripple in this sea, a current felt most deeply by family and loved ones before radiating in exponential and unfathomable ways through all mankind. I hold little hope for an afterlife, but perhaps this echoing of days well-lived is heaven enough.

I head home. I'll brew another cup of coffee and revisit my eulogy. There is time, and while I will never pin down the words in my heart, I can at least make them shine a little brighter. ❧

PIKE by Benjamin Whitmer

Owen Hill

"I think crime fiction is almost like a product of capitalism. It's about social inequality."
Ian Rankin

If America ever sees a successor to Steinbeck (and we need one), I think he or she will come up through noir. What we call "literary fiction" can't seem to grapple with the silenced near-majority that makes up the underclass: the unemployed, the underemployed, the dirt poor. MFA infused journals, the *New Yorker*, and mainstream publishers mostly address the problems of the "middle class."

The Indy presses, especially those with crime fiction lines, offer a tougher alternative to the soft focus "problems of the rich" aspect of mainstream fiction. If you want to read smart and you're willing to look around, the scene is teeming with Steinbecks, Zolas, Dreisers. . .except that their work usually involves a murder. Although come to think of it those other guys dealt with murder, too. Maybe they were writing genre.

My nomination for the Next Steinbeck award is Benjamin Whitmer. His first novel, *Pike* (PM Press, Oakland) is plenty tough, as you'd expect from noir. But it's more than that.

He won't let us believe that his characters are losers. Beaten down, prone to quick violence, but not without dignity. Whitmer draws them with great heart and a lack of pretension. You won't exactly like these characters. *Pike* has a coiled snake quality, Wendy makes me shudder with the depth of her anger, and the others are surrounded by thieves and perverts. You will come to some understanding if you pay attention. And, forgive the word but there is a *universal* quality there—what they do to survive is what we all do, or will do when circumstances turn against us.

All good crime writing must have a sense of place—Hammet's San Francisco, Chandler's LA, and so on. Whitmer brings us to the slums of Cincinnati. Neighborhoods like this don't get written about much anymore. Whitmer nails it with a painful elegance:

> The Long Drop Center is the first place you look when you go hunting for bums especially if it's wintertime and the bum's a junky.
> So says Bogie. The staff makes a policy of not bothering to check the bathrooms when it's cold out. Unlike most of the other charitable spots in Cincinnati, they'd rather bums get high on their toilet than turn into an icicle in some alley.

Grave, but precise and in its way, poetic. I can't imagine this appearing in a *Review* or a *Quarterly*. But, then, where would Steinbeck publish now? Perhaps in crime fiction magazines. ❧

Cauliflower Soup

Peter Schireson

I try and get it right,
how you love the cauliflower soup
in that little Italian place uptown
with dark red walls
and the grumpy old maitre d'
with cauliflower ears, and how
it's those ears that help me recall
your beloved cauliflower soup.

But then you remind me
it's actually brussels sprouts
you order uptown,
that the walls
aren't dark red, that's
a different spot, and that
the maitre d' must be from a time
and place before we ever met,
if he's real at all.

You're right, of course, right
about everything, and I see
I've bent another indelible line
you've drawn with the ink
of time and place,
and that I can't be trusted
not to order cauliflower soup for you.

And at the same time
I am very fond of the old maitre d'
with the cauliflower ears,
grumpy as he is.

Storm Damage

Peter Schireson

I'm going to bed without skin,
only tendons and muscles,
aching, done-in by my own words.
Under the sheet, still hot
from a fire I lit and fed,
I dream up a storm to cool myself off,
and in the no-time of dreamtime,
drains overflow, the ground runs
out of shapes to hold the rain,
it's water on water
and wind against walls,
old nails creak in purlins
where the planks are weak,
the moon breaks the curtains
and crawls across the floor
to where in the light
though not a kneeling man
I'm kneeling now.

Seeds Like Teeth

Delaney Nolan

He couldn't stop spilling oranges everywhere he went. When he was five, he was a hide-and-seek failure, when an orange always rolled out from under the slide or tilted open a closet door. When he went to the grocery store with his mother, he always had a wrist slapped when they left, because she reached for his hand and the sinister fruit would drop and spin serenely across the parking lot. He always apologized, looking at his shoes, confused.

It wasn't until elementary school that it became a problem. By fifth grade, his mother was suspicious, because there were no orange trees in Brooklyn, but the kitchen always smelled sweet and the fruit bowls were always overflowing. She wanted him to talk to a therapist, for his kleptomania.

"Where are they coming from?"

"I don't know. They just come."

Middle school was the worst part. At the same time as the reedy boys around him began to shoot up and trip over the ladders of their own voices, he heard snickers when oranges rolled down the back of his jacket and spun out onto the floor. He stooped. It got worse. They fell out of his pockets when he walked. They fell out of his sweaty hand when he met a new girl. Once in the boy's bathroom, a tenth-grader with oily skin whose father shot at dogs held him against a wall and shook him hard while oranges filled his tucked in shirt and fell out his cufflinks. Others stood around and gawked. They called him a freak, or obsessed, or queer. One boy would only call him a commie, but that still bothered him.

It got a little better after that. Eighth grade was the worst, but after that he got a little keener. His family knew by then, and so did he. It stuck in his mind and sat there though, made camp, painted on his brain-cave-walls so it was a part of him forever: he was the boy orange tree, and he would be.

His mother never took him to the doctor and he never bothered to go. It was very clear what was wrong. It was very clear medical technology had never encountered this exact problem and would not be able to fix it. He had enough of being a freakshow, sideshow, carnival, weird-o. He suffered through high school by spending lunches on the sidewalk benches, smoking cloves, and wearing baggy jeans. He threw citrus at cars where they exploded meatily like a punch landing. If one stopped to yell, he would yell back nonsense and feel like a hero.

"What's wrong with you, buddy?!"

"Buddy! Your car hit my orange! Man! Get out! Hey! Blockhead! Thief! Commie! Gringo! Pedophile!" until they drove away.

He ate alone. He ate mostly vegetables.

Sometimes he tried to eat dirt. It felt good but it dried his mouth out and tasted too coppery, so he spit it out in clumps.

When he was in college it wasn't too bad. He was okay with waking up early to empty his sheets out the fifth floor window, aiming for the dumpster. His roommate only liked computers and didn't care about "his fruit thing." They had conversations. Girls in fraternity basements told him he smelled like their mother and bared their teeth. Sometimes one would kiss him:

Her face would loom in like a crashing zeppelin—and then, after a beat she would jerk back with her hands on her mouth and her earrings swinging:

"Is your mouth full of twigs? Or something?"

He joined a lot of clubs, and he sat in the back during meetings. He had friends, but they were distant ones. He went to classes that weren't his and listened to professors talk. They asked him questions and he gave long, abstract answers full of "subjectively" and "liminal time-space" and "societal repercussions," while they nodded, and he didn't know what he was saying and he wasn't ever right or wrong. He took long showers and kept his desk neat and looked busy. He wrote a lot of bad poetry.

On graduation day he got a little bit drunk on champagne at 11 AM and took pictures with his parents. He thought about the freshman he'd been and how embarrassing that person was. It was sweltering, and the sun made everyone squint and duck a little. He felt hot and nauseous when an orange rolled out his long robe sleeve and over the chancellor's liver-spotted hand and under the podium. Four more fell on his way off stage. Some boys in the audience thought that it was a joke. They laughed or whooped. He skipped the after-parties.

He moved to Seattle and got a job, working the phones for the technical help department of a computer software company. He liked his job okay. He liked to picture his customers, and sometimes he imagined he could hear in their voice some camaraderie of freakishness, like a hook hand, or a peg leg, or a little tail. He always told them his real name. One day an old lady called; she sounded white, in her eighties maybe, and he imagined her grown son was paying for her but not visiting.

"Well, I just don't think this computer business is for me." She said with a cheery sigh after a few minutes.

"Is there anything else I can help you with, ma'am?"

"Oh aren't you gracious." When she breathed in she held the phone too close to her mouth and it sounded like a sail filling. "You know, I am about to make some chicken and mashed potatoes. It's been a long time but it's for a special occasion. You've been very helpful. Now I hope you go home and have a nice hot meal and a good squeeze, okay?"

"Okay. Have a good night ma'am." And she hung up.

He could have a hot meal at home. He had a kitchen full of baking ingredients. But they all ended up tasting to him sweet, and tangy, and too long in the sun. He started to think about his kitchen when he hung up. There were some dishes in the sink. He thought about them, and then he thought about the dishes in the sink last night, and tomorrow night, and about how he needed to buy new pillowcases, and then about the fat waddling Mormon who lived below him, and about the fat men in the cubicles around him, and all their tired faces, and so after work he went to a bar.

He never went to bars, had never really tried to go to bars. He felt sure that they would remind him of eighth grade. Now he went to the bar and discovered he was right. He wore a leather jacket because it made him feel safe. He sat on the corner like in the movies and ordered whiskey and water. He drank one, and then he ordered another, and he drank another and one more until he was drunk. He saw a woman in a dark green dress sit at the bar. The air wobbled like he was looking through an aquarium. His head felt soft and made of chicken fat. He had another whiskey and water. Then he stood up and walked to the green dress and sat on the stool next to it. The woman looked at him. He was scared and sweating and it was hard to look at her eyes. She had high cheekbones and sharp eyebrows that made her seem feline. Her upper lip was line-thin and she had a cluster of freckles just above her right brow like a gorgeous mistake. He decided he was in love with her.

"Hello." She smiled at him uncertainly.

He opened his mouth and choked as an orange, ripe and dimpled and shining, rolled out of his mouth and onto her lap, slick with spit.

"Oh God! What is wrong with you?" She jumped up disgusted, and fled backwards. The thick sweaty bartender was rolling his eyes at him.

"Sorry," he grumbled drunkenly and emptied his pockets onto the bar and walked out the door.

"Hey!" Yelled the bartender. "You can't leave your goddamned fruit in here!"

"My goddamned fruit." He mumbled, climbing to the street.

That was when he began to get really angry. Oranges, he would think to himself. Why does it have to be those goddamned oranges. He wondered, why it had to be only that one fruit, all the time. Why not strawberries, patient and cheerful under their little green caps, or pears with their tempting swells. He wanted to smell cherries in the morning, or feel the fuzz of a kiwi down his spine like a tickle. Even blueberries, bruise-purple and staining his clothes, or lemons, sharp and bright and starry. A pomegranate to hold him in hell with its glossed ruby guts, or guavas, tender and exotic, or grapes with their lucent skin, quivering on the bunch. Or apples, honestly, the most visceral and holy of them all. He began to dream of it. He dreamt of any other food. When he dreamt, the colors were muted. When he woke up, he spit out seeds like teeth.

Once he tried to drown in them. He didn't think about it very hard. He skipped work and lay on his back on his living room floor and stared up at the constellation of plaster nubs on the ceiling. Every once in a while he felt an orange's solid weight in his palm, and he would lift the heel of his hand just enough so that the ball would roll lazily like a sigh just past his fingertips. He lay there for hours and hours, until he got hungry and had to pee and he got up and ate Indian leftovers at the breakfast nook, glaring at the shallow, lurid puddle covering his carpet. He didn't try again.

He went back to work and later decided it was a very freshman thing to do.

Then after years and years he met Alicia. He met her at a gas station. He was grown and barely talked to his parents anymore. She was stuck there with an old rusting Ford that would only choke and cough. She was tall and slim and had straight bangs. When she spoke, he swore the words fell out of her mouth like jewels. They were both on their way back into the city. He surprised himself and offered a ride. She thanked him, and made small talk for a while, and then she began to doze because she was exhausted. She leaned her seat back and peered lazily through half-closed eyes.

Later she tried to tell him this: sun, sifting dust through the air around her and catching it in amber. It was low and turned everything the color of old film. Trees they passed chopped it up into staccato notes. The lining of the roof was red and sagging, and put a soft border above. A fish-shaped piece of glass hung by twine from the rear-view mirror and caught the light, which spangled and leaped like ballet. He was just barely humming Dooley Wilson. The soft-spun glow and the roof like a tongue and the light dancing and the tangy smell in the car, like waking up to windchimes, made her feel bitter-sweet and powerless and glad, like her muscles could have turned to cream. Later, she said, she decided then, half-asleep, that she was going to marry him. He dropped her off at home and an orange fell in her lap and he blushed. She thought it was sweet and gave him her number.

He couldn't even hide it through their first date. She laughed at his shy jokes and let him put his hands on hers. But Alicia realized what he was when they took the subway home, and she saw him cough and grimace and loosen his collar, and an orange, tinted green and with a tiny twig still attached, bloomed from the hollow of his throat, and he fumbled it out of his hands to the dirty ribbed floor, where it knocked against the shoes of an old Jewish woman peering firmly out the window. He bit his tongue and it tasted sugary. But Alicia just smiled at him, and kissed him right between his collar bones, right there in the train, and he felt knots loosen and come undone behind his shoulder blades where the stems of wings would have been. He was so happy he didn't know what to do.

She didn't mind and she didn't ask for an explanation. She told him she grew up in a commune but he didn't really know what that meant. She began to love him for the crinkles around his eyes. When they slept together the first time, only one or two soft spheres skied down his spine and thumped softly. He kissed her and she felt velvety and dark, like elegant words in a new language. She pushed her fingers through his hair and came back with a handful of soft, small white petals, some torn and bleeding faintly pink juice. She breathed on them and they scattered.

She said, "You're the real thing."

When they woke up, the bed was littered with little ripped flowers. It looked like a snowstorm for a dollhouse, and the sheets were rosy and marbled.

So they lived gladly together in his small loft. Sometimes she gathered sacks full of just-rotting fruit and carried it to a compost site somewhere uptown, where they could help other things grow. They could have given them to the homeless veterans behind their building, and sometimes he did, but it felt too wrong and hurt his stomach. He was grateful for what she did, and for accepting it all, but she just said, "It's New York. If it weren't oranges it would be something else."

Sometimes in the mornings she sat outside in an Oxford shirt and smoked and pressed her lips to the tops of her knees, and he loved her for that, too.

They wanted children but could only bear to talk about it in small voices. One day he came home to Alicia looking pink and excited. She put their hands on her stomach and told him and he felt all the planets swing wildly on the end of their mobile.

They bought a crib. They bought a book about pregnancy with anatomical diagrams in it that he said looked like a map of Venice. They talked about finding a new place.

"With two rooms. Maybe even somewhere with a yard. Far away from train tracks."

"We'll see. Let's wait a little longer." Even then he knew. His cave-brain knew.

And another month later it happened. This time when he came home she was sitting against the wall and her hands were resting on the floor as tiny unwheeled carriages. She told him about the doctor, the disaster. Her head was leaned back like grief was pouring down her throat.

He lay on the living room carpet where he had tried half-heartedly to drown once and put his head in her hands. After a few minutes he felt the weight of the fruit resting against the bridge of his nose. Alicia was crying. He sat up and turned and knelt against the wall, with his forehead to it like he was praying, and picked up the tender globe, turning it over in his hands. He pressed his thumbs to it until the nails pierced the leathery rind, dug both in hungrily and pulled, the strings of pulp and pith splitting, juice running down his wrists, seeds slipping from under the pads of his thumbs. It was a deep, dawn of time red, one he had never seen before. He handed one half to his wife, who bent forward and closed her eyes, and pressed it to her face, and pressed it to her lips, and kissed it, and cried.

They still lived. They lived long lives. Alicia died of an aneurysm at eighty-two. They were watching a bad Lifetime movie when it happened. He wasn't surprised but he still looked around the room like he could find where she'd gone. There were people at the ceremony he had never met. He had her cremated and gave the urn to her college roommate to take to the Indian Ocean, like she'd wanted. It was just carbon, he thought. He still had her pictures, the small things she left behind in a drawer by the bed.

He lived two years longer. He began to go blind. When he knew he was dying he took a train out of the city, got off at a stop with a nice round name, and walked. He walked with a cane. It was fall. The wind was crisp and smelt like rot and wood smoke. It had just rained and the air felt clear and honest and he thought about the worms coming up out of the dirt. Fruit fell from his overcoat and lay dented in the new city.

He found woods, and deeper in them a low hill, and he lay down and drew leaves over himself and closed his eyes and went to sleep. It was easy. He felt warm and heard wind. He lay there undiscovered for months. Winter stormed in with all her queenly bluster and pomp and retreated again. The light came back. When the snow began to melt, a slim and twisting tree unfurled itself from where he was buried. Its branches spanned the pale yawning sky; it stretched to the still natal sun, plunging ropey roots down hungrily, and in the spring, it bloomed, it bloomed, it bloomed. ❧

They're All The Same Except They're All Different

Jim Hett

ONE DAY I TOOK A PIECE OF PAPER AND DECIDED TO FILL IT WITH DRAWINGS. WHEN I FINISHED, IT LOOKED FINE AND I TAPED IT TO THE WALL. LATER, I TOOK ANOTHER PIECE OF PAPER AND FILLED IT WITH DESCRIPTIONS OF WHAT I HAD JUST DRAWN. I TAPED IT TO THE WALL, TOO. THERE, SIDE BY SIDE, I HAD TWO THINGS THAT WERE EXACTLY THE SAME, YET TOTALLY DIFFERENT. I HAVE CREATED ADDITIONAL PIECES BY APPLYING VARIATIONS TO THE ORIGINAL DRAWINGS. THE IMAGES ARE HAND DRAWN. THE PAPER IS STANDARD LETTER SIZE COPY PAPER. THEY ARE PLACED IN COMMON FRAMES TO PROTECT THEM WHEN THEY ARE DISPLAYED. THE FRAMES DRAW LITTLE ATTENTION TO THEIR PERIMETERS AND DO LITTLE TO VISUALLY SEPARATE THEM FROM THEIR SURROUNDINGS. THE PICTURED OBJECTS AND DESCRIPTIONS WERE DRAWN FROM MY MEMORY AND IMAGINATION. I AM A MALE CAUCASIAN IN HIS MID-FORTIES, FROM THE NEW YORK CITY METROPOLITAN AREA, WORKING ON THESE DRAWINGS AT THE DAWN OF THE TWENTY FIRST CENTURY. THE DRAWINGS FILL A PAGE AND REPRESENT A WIDE VARIETY OF THINGS. THEY EMPHASIZE NO PARTICULAR THING OR POINT OF VIEW. THE DESCRIPTIONS ARE EXPLICIT, SUCCINCT AND LIKE THE DRAWINGS, FILL THE PAGE. THE ORIGINAL DRAWINGS SERVE AS A BASE. I TRACE THEM TO MAKE NEW PIECES. NEW PIECES ARE CREATED BY APPLYING VARIATIONS TO THEIR PREDECESSORS. THE VARIATIONS ARE CULLED FROM OBSERVATION AND IMAGINATION. THEY VARY BY MEDIA, CONTENT, STYLE, AND CONTEXT. THEIR VARIATIONS CAN ALSO VIOLATE THESE DESCRIPTIONS. THE PERCEPTION OF THE PIECES VARIES ACCORDING TO THE VIEWER. EACH PIECE IS ENTITLED TO IMPLY ITS VARIATION. THIS PIECE'S TITLE IS "DESCRIPTION OF THE WORK". THE GROUP IS ENTITLED ACCORDING TO A VIEWER'S COMMENT, "THEY'RE ALL THE SAME, EXCEPT THEY'RE ALL DIFFERENT." I GROUP AND ARRANGE PIECES TO CREATE PATTERNS. THE VARIATIONS CAN BE DISCERNED BY COMPARING INDIVIDUAL PIECES. I CONSIDER HOW AND WHERE THEY ARE DISPLAYED. I HOPE YOU ENJOY IT.

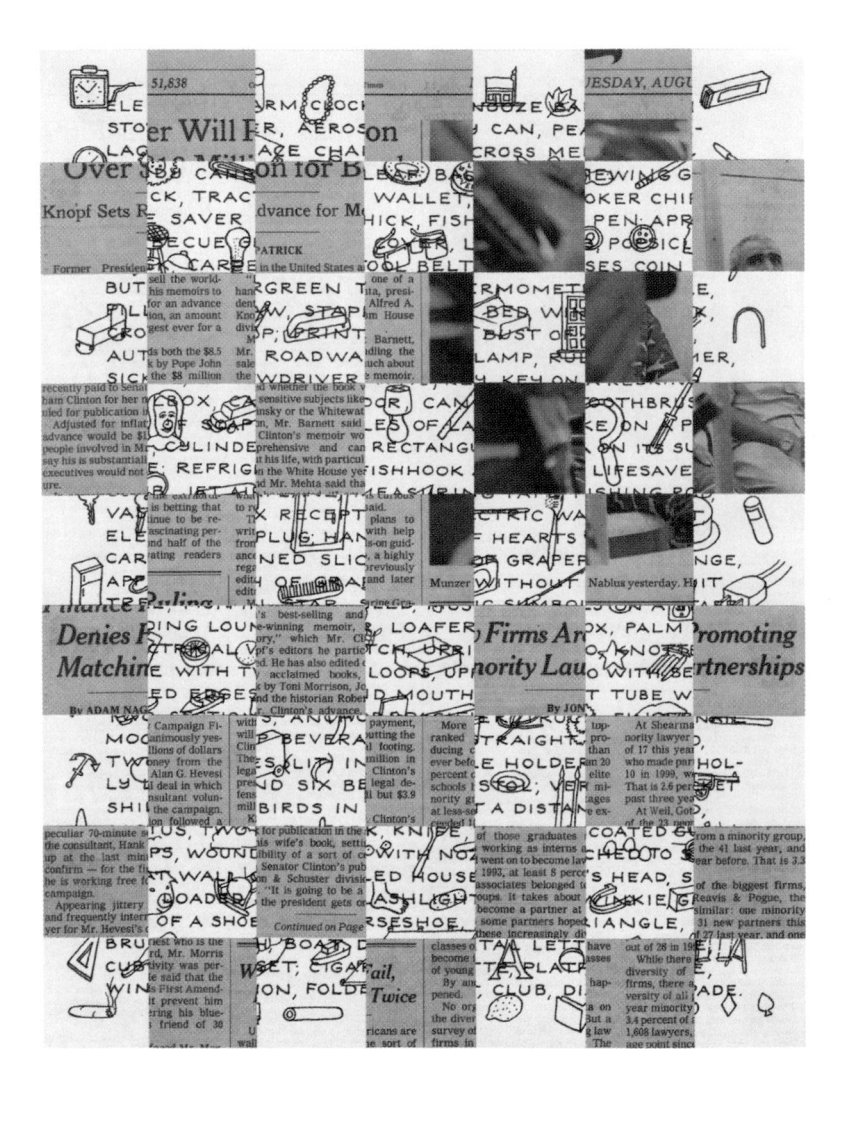

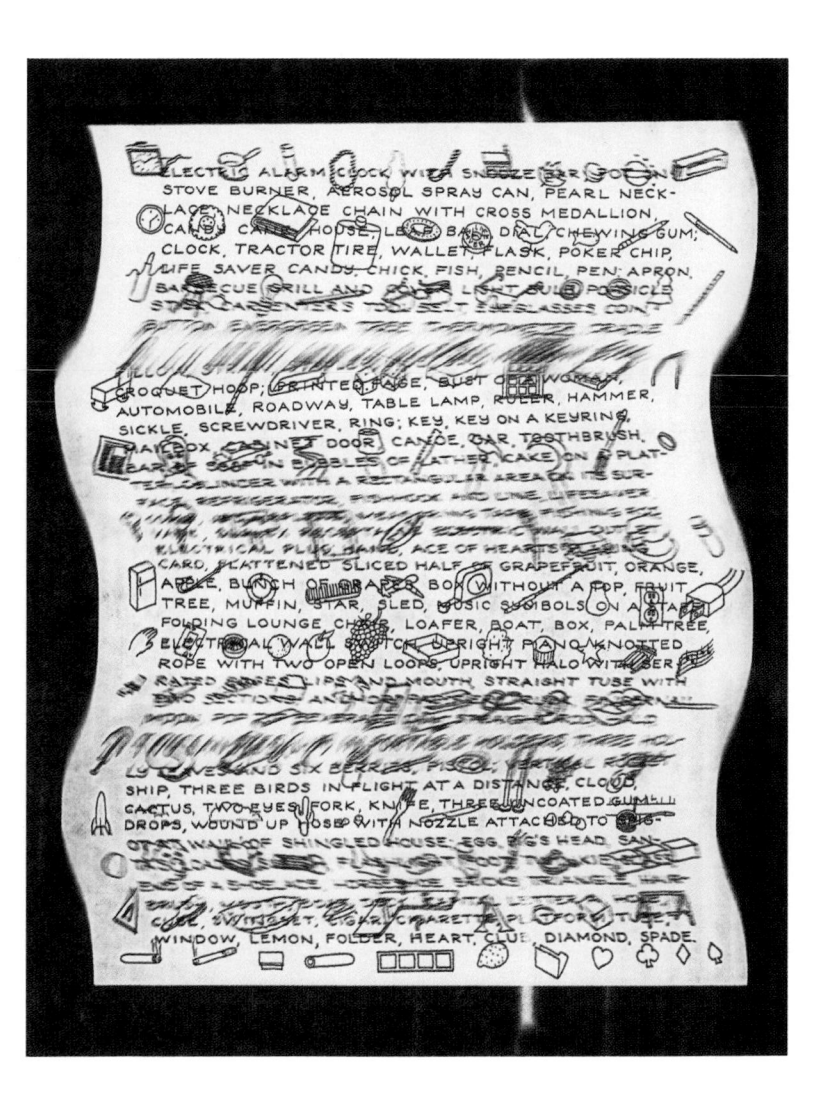

ELECTRIC ALARM CLOCK WITH SNOOZE BAR, POT ON
STOVE BURNER, AEROSOL SPRAY CAN, PEARL NECK-
LACE, NECKLACE CHAIN WITH CROSS MEDALLION,
CANDY CANE, HOUSE, LEAF, BALL, DIAL, CHEWING GUM,
CLOCK, TRACTOR TIRE, WALLET, FLASK, POKER CHIP,
LIFE SAVER CANDY, CHICK, FISH, PENCIL, PEN, APRON,
BARBECUE GRILL AND COVER, LIGHT BULB, POPSICLE
STICK, CARPENTER'S TOOL BELT, EYEGLASSES, COIN,
BUTTON, EVERGREEN TREE, THERMOMETER; CRADLE,
PILLOW, STRAW, STAPLER, DICE, BED, WINDOW, BOOK,
CROQUET HOOP, PRINTED PAGE, BUST OF A WOMAN,
AUTOMOBILE, ROADWAY, TABLE LAMP, RULER, HAMMER,
SICKLE, SCREWDRIVER, RING; KEY, KEY ON A KEYRING,
MAILBOX, CABINET DOOR, CANOE, OAR, TOOTHBRUSH,
BAR OF SOAP IN BUBBLES OF LATHER, CAKE ON A PLAT-
TER, CYLINDER WITH A RECTANGULAR AREA ON ITS SUR-
FACE, REFRIGERATOR, FISHHOOK AND LINE, LIFESAVER,
COMB, JET AIRPLANE, MEASURING TAPE, FISHING ROD,
VASE, DUPLEX RECEPTACLE ELECTRIC WALL OUTLET,
ELECTRICAL PLUG HAND, ACE OF HEARTS PLAYING
CARD, FLATTENED SLICED HALF OF GRAPEFRUIT, ORANGE,
APPLE, BUNCH OF GRAPES, BOX WITHOUT A TOP, FRUIT
TREE, MUFFIN, STAR, SLED, MUSIC SYMBOLS ON A STAFF;
FOLDING LOUNGE CHAIR, LOAFER, BOAT, BOX, PALM TREE,
ELECTRICAL WALL SWITCH, UPRIGHT PIANO, KNOTTED
ROPE WITH TWO OPEN LOOPS, UPRIGHT HALO WITH SER-
RATED EDGES, LIPS AND MOUTH, STRAIGHT TUBE WITH
TWO SECTIONS, ANCHOR, PACIFIER, TRUCK, FINGERNAIL
MOON, POP TOP BEVERAGE CAN, STRAIGHT ROD, HALO,
TWO CANDLES (LIT) IN PORTABLE HOLDERS, THREE HOL-
LY LEAVES AND SIX BERRIES; PISTOL, VERTICAL ROCKET
SHIP, THREE BIRDS IN FLIGHT AT A DISTANCE, CLOUD,
CACTUS, TWO EYES, FORK, KNIFE, THREE UNCOATED GUM-
DROPS, WOUND UP HOSE WITH NOZZLE ATTACHED TO SPIG-
OT AT WALL OF SHINGLED HOUSE, EGG, PIG'S HEAD, SAN-
TA'S LOADED SLEIGH, FLASHLIGHT, FOOT, TWINKIE, GLASS,
END OF A SHOELACE, HORSESHOE, BRICKS; TRIANGLE, HAIR-
BRUSH, MOUTH, BOAT, DOCK, CAPITAL LETTER A, HOLE,
CUBE, SWINGSET; CIGAR, CIGARETTE, PLATFORM, TUBE,
WINDOW, LEMON, FOLDER, HEART, CLUB, DIAMOND, SPADE.

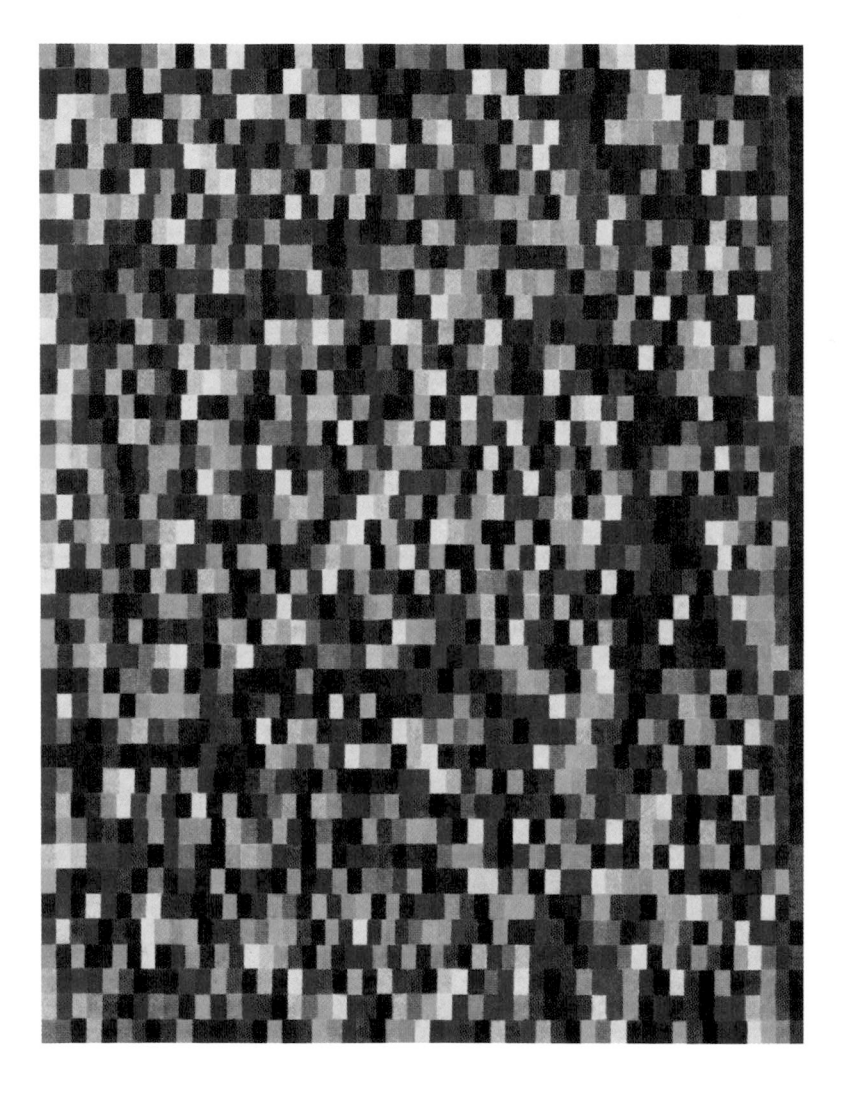

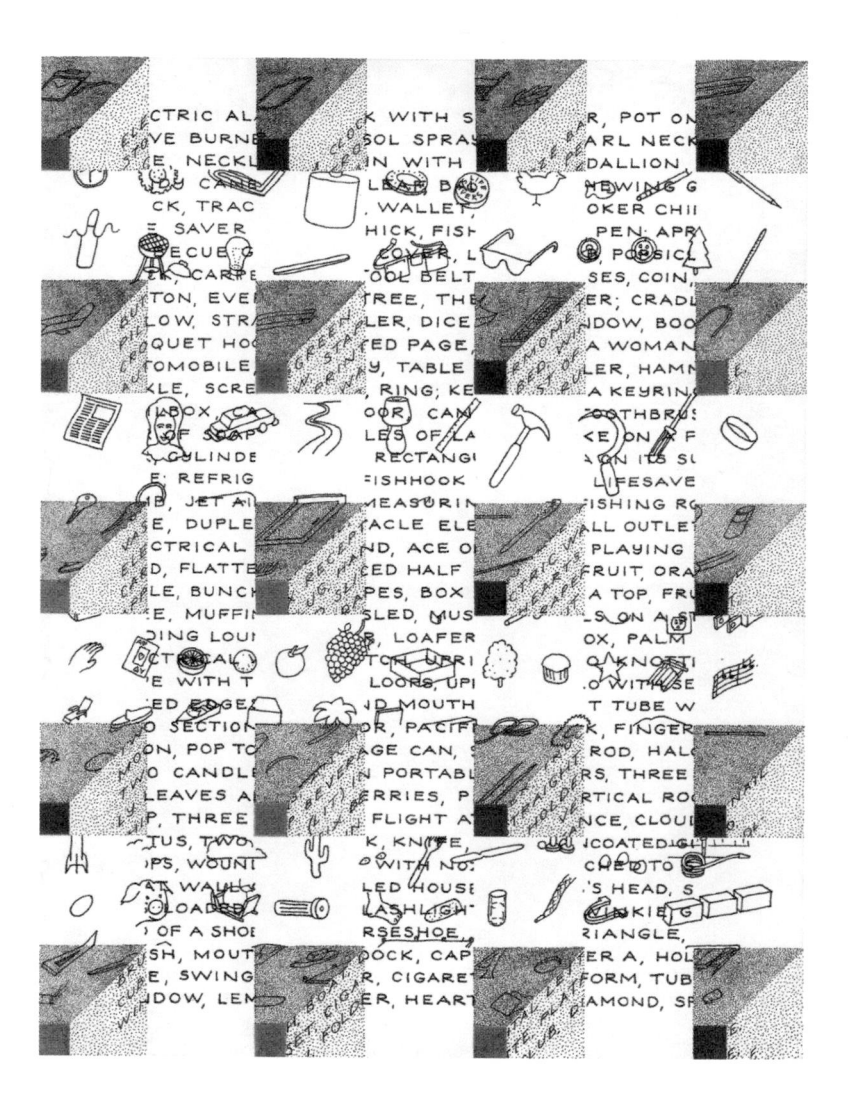

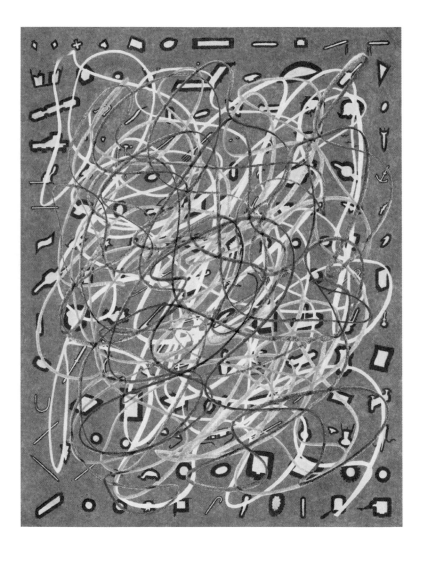

ELECTRIC ALARM CLOCK WITH SNOOZE BAR POT
STOVE BURNER AEROSOL SPRAY CAN PEARL NECK
LACE NECKLACE CHAIN WITH CROSS MEDALLION
CANDY CANE HOUSE LEAF BALL DIAL CHEWING G
CLOCK TRACTOR TIRE WALLET FLASK POKER CHI
LIFE SAVER CANDY CHICK FISH PENCIL PEN AP
BARBECUE GRILL AND COVER LIGHT BULB POPSI
STICK CARPENTER'S TOOL BELT EYEGLASSES CO
BUTTON EVERGREEN TREE THERMOMETER CRADLE
PILLOW STRAW STAPLER DICE BED WINDOW BOOK
CROQUET HOOP PRINTED PAGE BUST OF A WOMAN
AUTOMOBILE ROADWAY TABLE LAMP RULER HAMME
SICKLE SCREWDRIVER RING KEY KEY ON A KEYR
MAILBOX CABINET DOOR CANOE OAR TOOTHBRUSH
BAR OF SOAP IN BUBBLES OF LATHER CAKE ON
TER CYLINDER WITH A RECTANGULAR AREA ON I
FACE REFRIGERATOR FISHHOOK AND LINE LIFES
COME JET AIRPLANE MEASURING TAPE FISHING
VASE DUPLEX RECEPTACLE ELECTRIC WALL OUTL
ELECTRICAL PLUG HAND ACE OF HEARTS PLAYIN
CARD FLATTENED SLICED HALF OF GRAPEFRUIT
APPLE BUNCH OF GRAPES BOX WITHOUT A TOP F
TREE MUFFIN STAR SLED MUSIC SYMBOLS ON A
FOLDING LOUNGE CHAIR LOAFER BOAT BOX PALM
ELECTRICAL WALL SWITCH UPRIGHT PIANO KNOT
ROPE WITH TWO OPEN LOOPS UPRIGHT HALO WIT
RATED EDGES LIPS AND MOUTH STRAIGHT TUBE
TWO SECTIONS ANCHOR PACIFIER TRUCK FINGER
MOON POP TOP BEVERAGE CAN STRAIGHT ROD HA
TWO CANDLES LIT IN PORTABLE HOLDERS THREE

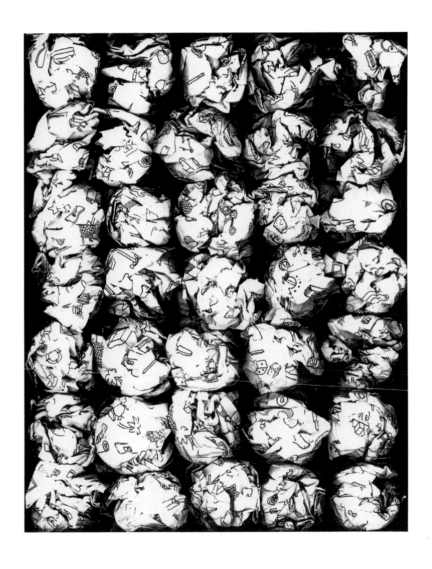

Jim Hett

The original images are 11" x 8.5".

Flight Perils

Sally Wen Mao

I.   [If I suffer, let it be in high places]

What, then, is the opposite of human?
Of girl?

           It swoops,   flies,
    retreats.
           Swift arc in the air: aerie
           to archipelago,
           dream arpeggios.

Once, I strung a wire
from my roof to yours. I walked that steel

thread with no parachute, just an umbrella,
    the wind threw a fit
    and I fell.   Carry me over

    this mountain blindfolded, dear one.
    The altitude hisses in my ears. Carry

    me on the palanquin of your body, leave
me on the silent ridge with the ruins
    of a jet crash. Metal wing hangs off its socket.

      The radio signal is broken
and so are my arms.
My hair is burning down
      but what I see

surprises me: behind dread, a lighthouse;
    behind mourning, a weathervane;
      behind the trees, a tiny skiff departing.

II. [Night swallowed all the juncos on Beacon Street]

The second death in my childhood
was a red-crested eagle, snagged
in cannon netting as it left its aerie
                    for the first time.

            I lived on this street. Overhead, a dozen juncos
            saw-toothed over marquisette.

3/4ths of a flock struck
in an electrical storm.

When I picked one up, its plume
                    showed no sign of lightning,
                    though its humerus bone

shattered to bits when touched.
Did they mistake the road
                    for a stream, boiling away
                    into the cloudy sea?

III. [Love the flightless, learn the dirt, live to stomp]

Once I read the story of a girl
who loved a flightless
creature.

        Leda, hurry and run,
        for your swan is waking.

In the cool willow, his fitful
grip surprised her. Her story bled
into its cloth. All the secrets in the dirt
reneged and built a bridge between enemies.

        What you need now is more than love.

At times I tromp the earth
searching for precision. As the sediment
flies away, I trust that worms still live here.
The suicidal swan walks into the tracks.

Sonnets for Kudryavka

Sally Wen Mao

Kudryavka, before Sputnik

Toast to you, dog, for your solar-powered
organs. Your smelt muscles sing. The slag
on your bones cannot die on this earth.
From dumpster to rocketship, the true
rags-to-riches tale—and it's not even
happening to a human. Not even happening
in America. World-famous gutter-sucker,
tonight you give birth to a new name: Laika.
Before any dog impregnates you, you will shoot
off into the galaxy. Mammal as asteroid,
ultimate runaway. Who are you, whose kismet
matches the greats—a martyr for thought,
like Socrates? Will you drink the hemlock
of space? You, Laika, original cosmonaut?

Kudryavka's Sobriquets

Zhuchka, little bug: stray mastiff covered
in snow—how many tulips have you eaten
since spring? How many cabbages drenched
in ruined milk? *Limonchik*, little lemon:
as a stray, you knew hunger so well you wrecked
your own mouth. In Moscow, they squeezed
lemons over your coat. The seeds stuck
to your damp fur, but the juice disinfected
you. As you licked your own neck, the taste sang
through your tongue. You howled and howled
and it opened your flesh and you were made
invincible. *Laika*, barker: you are that dog
whose face shined in red paint. You are that dog
they renamed so they can silence you again.

Kudryavka in the Capsule

If you had your way, you'd have traveled
the world on tour. Tongue wagging out,
you'd have felt the siroccos squirming
over your fur, the waters of clear brooks
softening it. You'd have tasted the meats
of animals you could never outrun. You'd
have chased them anyway, across mesas,
icescapes – the reindeer, you'd have gnawed
their fuzzy antlers. Gentle admirers would
pet you, take you in their arms. But now,
nothing sheathes your spinning aorta.
The clock runs faster than your legs
at their hungriest. You are strapped to drill
into oblivion, impale it like a breathing rapier.

Kudryavka: Liftoff

Shuttered in hot light & oil-seared stars,
you alone carry the weight of planetary
anxieties. The heat rises and your skeleton
quivers. A vatic singsong proclaims onslaught.
You panic but eat. It is a sticky gel and not
the mutton you were fed yesterday.
But yesterday is extinguished, and even
today and tomorrow have kidded you,
escaped. You are alone with your coccydynia.
Your lungs plump. You cannot understand
the machine of your solitude, its axles,
its weights. Outside, there is the timber
galaxy. You wake to terror and lumber fast
into the death that's at least known.

The Place Called Mother

Melanie Unruh

When I was a child, my mother would disappear.

Sometimes she would actually leave, but more often it turned out that she was hiding somewhere at home. The summer I was thirteen, while I was staying with my father, she quietly withdrew from the world yet again. My parents had been divorced for less than a year, and when I spent time with my father, my mother would be alone in her apartment on the other side of town. No matter how many times I called, she wouldn't pick up the phone, so finally I just showed up at her place. When she didn't answer the door, I used my key. All of the lights were on. The apartment smelled like old take-out food: French fry oil, processed meat, and pizza sauce.

"Hello?" I called. No answer.

The bedroom was empty. She was nowhere, but I still felt unsettled, like I could sense her presence. I turned on the light in the bathroom and opened the shower curtain, as though this were a game of hide-and-seek and my mother might actually be standing there. My gaze was downcast and I opened and closed the curtain quickly, so all I saw was a freckled arm and a flash of her worn teal T-shirt. I stared down at the bathroom tile, trying to decide what should come next. What could I say or do in response to finding my mother, a grown woman, fully dressed and hiding from her only daughter inside a bone-dry shower?

But I don't remember what came next. It's startling to realize that such a moment is no longer a part of my memory. Wasn't *everything* riding on what happened next? Did I say her name? Did I just run away? Did she emerge from the shower, her light blue eyes fearful? Maybe we both did nothing. That seems to be something we've grown quite good at. What I do know is that now, every time I enter a bathroom, I'm both compelled and terrified to probe the closed shower curtain. Even if it's not my house. When I peel back the plastic and inevitably discover that the only contents of the shower are bright green bottles of shampoo and sodden loofahs, I breathe a sigh of relief. If they weren't prone to mold, I would never close another shower curtain as long as I live.

When I was five or six, my mother vanished altogether. No one saw her for days and her black hatchback sat in the driveway, untouched. I awoke in the middle of the night after the first day she'd been gone and peered down the blond wooden staircase into the kitchen. My father and my older brother Christopher were still awake, talking. Their expressions were grim when I descended the stairs. My father was on the phone, and he watched me with his dark eyes, as he tried not to say anything that might alert me that something was actually wrong. I sat at the kitchen table and peered up at them, a pair of tall males who I was beginning to recognize had no idea how to care for me in my mother's absence. Christopher put his hand on my shoulder, which scared me more than anything else. He was eight years older and I was used to him decapitating my Barbies and tricking me into watching scary movies. This quiet comfort implied something much bigger than us.

The following day I went next door to my grandparents' house after school. There was a policeman, tall and foreboding in his dark uniform, standing in the kitchen, questioning people. When was the last time anyone had seen her? Did she have a history of disappearing? Where might she have gone?

When they finally found her, I was confused and horrified. My father told me that she had to go away to a special hospital for awhile. I asked why. He told me that he had uprooted all the shoes and clothes from their closet floor and discovered her hiding in the back. She'd been gone for days; everyone had been searching for her, assuming the worst, and here she was the whole time inside her own bedroom closet. Even as a small child, I knew this wasn't a game. Mothers didn't disappear for days and then re-materialize inside of closets.

My mother was not well. She said that strange men had been trying to hurt her, so she had climbed into the back of the closet, covered herself with whatever she could find, and as a final step, to keep the men away if they should happen to discover her, she ripped out one of her front teeth.

It has taken me twenty years to find the words to express what it felt like, what it still feels like to imagine my mother in such a state. What must have been going through her mind? How does your life ever get to the point where you are curled in a ball in the dark, hiding within reach of your own family?

When she finally came home from the hospital, she told me about her experience.

She said, "I thought those men were coming to get me."

"But why didn't you ask for help if there were men in our house, Mommy?"

"Because they weren't really there."

My mother is bipolar. She is not the caricatured manic-depressive, buying a yacht on her credit card one day and slashing her wrists the next. She's what doctors refer to as a "slow cycler," meaning that she can be in a deep depression for four or five years before the mania, which usually only lasts a few months, sets in. Although the highs are brief, they are startling. I won't have talked to her in months, and she won't have done a single proactive thing in years, when suddenly my phone begins to ring nonstop.

The fall of my junior year in college was my busiest semester ever: I was working two on-campus jobs, doing a full course load, taking the train from Rider University in New Jersey into New York City every week for an internship, planning my best friend's bridal shower, preparing to leave for a semester abroad in Spain, and trying to end a four and a half year relationship with my boyfriend, Mark.

Out of the blue, my mother called me. She never initiated contact. It was always me reaching out, and most times, these attempts went without acknowledgment. I'm sure if there were a collection of all the unanswered messages that I've left for my mother over the years, they would range anywhere from outraged to hysterical to stoic in tone.

"I'm feeling great," she told me.

"Really?" I tried to contain my shock. The last time I remembered my mother being well was my junior year in high school. I knew she had slipped under the radar again when she failed to come see me before I left for my first prom. The pictures from both proms are of me standing between my father and my stepfather, Bob. The first year, my best friend Laurel's mother helped us get ready, fussing with the camera, with the coordinated placement of our dates' boutonnieres. Her eyes filled with tears when she saw us descend the stairs together, our feet loud and unsteady in our high heels. Laurel's mother was in the video; she was in the pictures. She was there.

My mother took a deep breath on the other end of the phone. "I'm seeing a psychiatrist and I'm taking medication again and I've been out walking every day on the road—and I've been talking to my sisters and my mom and I'm looking for a job—I might start working at the Y—and I've been cleaning the house and I want to come see you at school—I'm sorry I've never been to your school—and I can't reach your brother—not that I'm surprised or blame him—and I think Bob doesn't know what to do now that I won't stop talking—I put a sign on the bedroom door to remind me not to start talking his ear off as soon as he wakes up at five and just wants to write in his journal—"

A week later she called to tell me that it was almost Grandparents Day and she thought I should let my grandparents know that *I* remembered, so she'd bought me a card and taken it to Mark's house, so I could mail it that weekend when I went to see him.

After this high, my mother leveled out and was doing well for a little over a year before she crashed again.

Sometimes, the only way I can find out about my mother is by calling my father. I'm forced to go this route because my father and my stepfather, Bob work together as general contractors and because Bob doesn't know how to check the voicemail at home, to see whose calls they've been missing because my mother has turned the ringer off.

Most times, my father will just give Bob the phone and I can bypass having to talk with my father about my mother's condition. But recently, I hadn't heard from either my mother or stepfather in months, so I called my father. Bob wasn't with him.

"How's she doing?" I asked, cringing at the idea that he was my conduit to this information.

"I think she's the same. She hasn't worked or left the house much in a year."

I knew this, but somehow I expected to hear something different.

"She needs to go back on medication, but she has to be the one who wants it."

I bit my lip, as a familiar tightness seized my chest. If I spoke then, I knew I'd start crying, so I let him continue, repeating the words that have become a well-worn script throughout the course of my life.

Memories of her hospitalizations crept back into my consciousness and before I could stop myself, I said, "But what about before when she used to go to the hospital? I mean, that hasn't happened in a long time. Would something like that even help?"

He sighed. "Well, I don't know if you ever knew this, but your mother tried to commit suicide a few times. Those were the times she went to the hospital."

Of course, I knew this. I knew she went to the hospital and I knew that she tried to commit suicide, but somehow I never put together the fact that they were so intertwined. My mind was flooded. I struggled to recall exactly how many times she was institutionalized when I was a child. If I could remember this number, then I would know exactly how many times she had tried to kill herself and I could draw a more concrete map of our past, of all the times she almost disappeared from the story. I was glad to finally have this piece of my mother's puzzle. But at the same time, I was angry at him for telling me in such a patronizing tone. Why was *he* the keeper of this information?

As my father went on, I thought of a time years ago when he and I were driving somewhere on Route 202 just outside West Chester, Pennsylvania. I think the road remains so vivid to me because I had to stare out the window to keep from screaming at him. We were coming off an overpass, and as the ramp uncoiled before us, my father opened a wound inside me that I didn't even realize existed: "You know, if your mother hadn't gotten sick, we would probably still be married."

I can't begin to understand what my father went through being married to my mother for almost twenty-five years. I do know that while she struggled with her illness, he found comfort in the arms of other women, and that her inability to stay well ultimately ended their marriage. Or did it? Sometimes I wonder if all of us, my father included, have used my mother's illness as a scapegoat for our own weaknesses.

There are days when I want to shake my mother and demand to know how she can keep doing this to herself and her family. I still have to remind myself not to look at her condition as something black and white. No one would bat an eyelash if I said she was diabetic or had Parkinson's. But as soon as I say she's bipolar, people act strangely. Some tell me that they also know someone who's bipolar—a neighbor or a cousin—and I want to hit them. My mother raised me to be a pacifist, but sometimes I tremble with rage at people who don't understand that when your mother is the one with a mental illness, it's not something you can just talk about offhand or use to one-up the other person. Most people get extremely awkward. A pained expression crosses their faces and they grow quiet, unsure of what to say to the daughter of a crazy person.

I briefly dated a guy who wanted to know all about my mother and her illness. His morbid curiosity was tedious, to say the least.

"So where is your mother now?" he asked, as we lay in bed one night.

"Delaware," I said, turning to face the wall.

"Okay, so what's she doing?"

"Nothing," I said.

He laughed. "She can't be doing nothing. She has to be—"

"She's not."

I'm haunted by a question that most people say in jest: *Will I become my mother?*

Everyone has their highs and lows, but I scrutinize mine, looking for clues that I might be going too far one way or the other. My mind often feels as though it operates like tabbed internet browsing; if I don't do everything all at once, I feel unproductive. I have a hard time prioritizing and not jumping from task to task. As I write this, I'm also doing laundry, listening to music and singing along, checking two of my email accounts, researching, examining the clothes I'm wearing for stains, thinking about texting a friend and needing to feed my cat, writing a blog, and deciding what to pack for my lunch tomorrow. Is this just low-level mania? Sometimes I function well doing many things at once, but do I have the self-awareness to know if it got to be too much?

My depression scares me more. It can be much more tangible, and since that's the way my mother's illness works, I worry that could be an indicator that I'm just as ill. In college, I was once clinically depressed for months. I was twenty and had just transferred to my third new school in three years. I felt as though if I didn't make it work there, I was doomed to never finish. Everything felt wrong: my sleep was erratic, I could barely eat, and I started having panic attacks.

Was my depression just situational? I don't know. What I do know is that in the midst of it, I devised a plan. If I got to the point where I couldn't handle it anymore, I was going to take a bottle of pills and climb into the trunk of my car. No take backs.

I never did buy pills or test the limits of my trunk. Instead, I thought of my mother, who at one point had seemed hard-wired for suicide attempts but who had transformed her desire to die into a general, fearful malaise when she realized what her death would have meant for her children. So I gritted my teeth and pushed through it.

But that nagging voice doesn't go away so easily: what if I *do* become her? The chances are high. Scientists believe that of all the psychiatric illnesses, bipolar disorder may be the one that is most closely tied to genetics. Some studies say that I have a 1 in 5 chance. Others say it's 15-30%. The thing is, *no one really knows*. I'd like to hope that regardless of what the odds actually are, I've beaten them by now. But will the children I want to have someday be so lucky? I could just end up being a carrier, a woman book-ended by her ill mother and child. Unless I outlive everyone, my entire life will have been spent steeped in their illnesses. It's not fair to say that I've paid my dues, but I feel like I deserve a mother-child relationship that doesn't get put on hold for years at a time.

I know I'm not immune to depression. There's no way to know for sure why it manifested itself in me how and when it did. Maybe there's a marker imprinted in my blood and that was just my year to hemorrhage. Maybe it's out of my system now and I'll never go there again. Or maybe twenty was the onset of my disease, whereas my mother's came sooner and louder when, at sixteen, she swallowed enough aspirin to make her violently ill, but not enough to take her before her lifelong battle would begin.

I'm forced to cycle with my mother, living hand-to-mouth on despair and hope. When she relapses into depression, the harrowing deflation of the hope I've allowed myself to feel is shocking, yet inevitable. A year and a half ago, when she lost all stability once again, I was crushed. Four and a half years of illness versus less than two years of wellness is a cruel trade-off.

But my mother is better than the person her illness makes her out to be. The disease degrades her. When she is well, she is someone who I can tell anything to. The summer before my junior year in college, I broke up with Mark for the penultimate time and without knowing where else to go, I drove to her house. She'd been exhibiting signs of a possible return—answering the phone and even calling me back—so I took a chance that she might be there for me.

When I got to her house, she was already dressed and had even combed her short white-blond hair. She made me a glass of chocolate milk and hugged me as I cried.

"I can't believe I just did that," I said, sitting back in my chair.

She said, "I'm not surprised."

"What do you mean?" I asked.

"I can't believe you stayed together this long," she said. "You were so young when you started dating and I never thought it was healthy for you to just be with him."

"How so?"

"Look at you. You keep trying to get out of here, but you always end up coming back because of him. He has no intention of going anywhere."

"I know," I said, turning my glass in my hands.

"What ever happened to your plan to live alone in an apartment with your cat before you got married?" she asked, smiling.

I rolled my eyes. "I was like ten when I said that."

"So?" she said, hands on her chubby hips. "It still sounds like a good idea."

"I guess. But I'm scared."

She frowned at me. "When did you get like this? When did you become a shrinking violet?"

I gave her a quizzical look. "A what?"

She sighed. "It's an expression. It just means that you're afraid of things."

I shrugged.

"You can do anything you want." She squeezed my hand. "Don't limit yourself."

The irony of her words was not lost on me.

When my mother stops taking medication, which she always does, everything crumbles. She doesn't forget to take it; she keeps a pill container labeled with the days of the week in her kitchen. She knows the consequences of missing her meds. But she is like clockwork. Every time a medication keeps her from gravitating towards either pole, she develops an invincibility complex. It's not the medication that's making her well, it's her willpower. She's a modern medical marvel! She alone must be the one bipolar person who has been able to conquer her disease all on her own.

It's fucking bullshit.

But whom do I blame? Is it the doctors who can't really force her to do anything? My mother and Bob hover just above the poverty level, so the doctors she does see are often state-appointed, and I suspect, somewhat inept. Without healthcare, she doesn't get treatment that promotes a consistent relationship with a doctor for any length of time.

Is Bob the culpable one then? He's lived alone with my mother and her disease for close to a decade. If it weren't for him, she would probably be living on the street somewhere. I don't know anyone else in my family as patient as him, myself included. It's not like he wants his wife to be sick. So how can I hold him accountable for not watching her every second, for not making her want a healthy life that at the end of the day, is maybe just too much for her to know what to do with?

I want to blame *her*, but how can I?

It was my mother's birthday this week. I went to the store to buy her a card, something I dread doing every year. Hallmark doesn't make cards for people who have strained relationships with their mothers. Their cards say things like, "For all that you've done and continue to do," or, "You are a shining example to all of us." I can't sign a lie and put it in the mail without feeling like a total phony. And so I began my usual search, trying to find that elusive, generic card that said little more than "Happy Birthday."

I cried in the middle of the grocery store, looking through these cards, not because the messages were so meaningful to me, but because I felt so disconnected from these mothers who were lovingly addressed in pink and yellow verses. Other people bought these cards every day without a second thought.

I finally selected a card and took it home, which was half the battle. Now I had to convince myself to send it. My brother told me that she forgot his birthday this year. Our birthdays are a straight shot: Christopher's in August, hers in September, and mine in October. Should I ignore hers because she'd blown off his and was likely to do the same with mine anyway? My twentieth birthday came and went without a word from her. It took me years to let that go, but I eventually did. But now that she had done it to Christopher, my anger rose again. She never even acknowledged my cards, so why bother? Why did I feel obligated to do something for her birthday anyway?

I mailed the card, but decided against calling. There was nothing to say.

I thought that would be the end of it. Another birthday, come and gone. The funny thing is that she ended up calling me. I couldn't even remember the last time we'd spoken on the phone. It had to have been months before. So on her son's birthday, she didn't call him, but on her own goddamned birthday *she called me*. We spoke for a minute, but I was in a meeting and said I'd have to call her back. She consented, but as I'd predicted, when I called back at the exact time that I said I would, she didn't answer.

Bob called several days later, to ask if I'd spoken to her on her birthday.

"Briefly," I said.

"Good," he said. "No one else even acknowledged it."

"Oh."

"It seemed like she might be thinking about hurting herself, but I think we're past that now."

I felt heartsick. Did my mother think that I was the only person on her side? What would she do if she knew what I thought, what I wrote about her?

I used to see a counselor who told me, "You need to be willing to accept the possibility that your mother may never be well again."

When my mother eventually climbed out of that particular depression, once again revealing the lovely person hiding beneath all that fear, I wanted to go back and find that counselor. I wanted to run up to her and tell her how wrong she'd been, that her fancy degree meant jack. My mother was just fine. She wanted to leave the house, to find a job, to exercise and eat healthy food, to call me several times a week so that she could once again be a part of my life. She was just like anyone else's mother. She was not the living dead; that was only a mask she wore sometimes, when the world became too much for her. Here was my *real* mother, who had finally freed herself and who was going to stay well because we had finally arrived at *THE LAST TIME*.

But it wasn't the last time. It's frightening to acknowledge the truth in those words: *Your mother may never be well again.* As in, even when she appears to be functional and engaged, it is only a matter of time before once again she is overcome.

My mother turned fifty-eight this year. As far as I know, she no longer climbs into closets and showers, in the hope that no one will see her. Regardless, she remains largely unseen. But for people like me, whether she is hiding or standing right out in the open, her presence is like a phantom limb. There are days when I have to remind myself that she is still alive. Sometimes I feel as though I could just reach out and touch her, but when my hands press for that space, for that place called mother, they rediscover the emptiness that is her void. ❧

SANCTUARY by William Faulkner

James Boice

Sanctuary is William Faulkner's whorish dalliance in genre, the Faulkner novel they won't teach you in school, the one no academic has made a career talking about at symposiums. It's about bootleggers, murder, set-ups, bizarre sexual proclivities, grotesquery, evil. It starts off with a college girl named Temple Drake, the daughter of a judge, in a car with a frat boy-type in the middle of nowhere Mississippi. He's drunk. They wreck. They go up to a big dark creepy house for help. Bootleggers are squatting there. The one in charge is named Popeye. He is an evil scary little man, to say the least. There is also a half-wit, a blind, deaf, and dumb old man, a hardboiled sometimes-prostitute. It's a horrifying little band of rednecks. Very *Texas Chainsaw Massacre*. A creepy baby is kept in a drawer. Meat cooks on the stove. They don't let the pretty college girl leave. Things only get weirder from there. And it's all portrayed with an unnerving level of sustained emotional intensity and effortlessly transcendent lyricism and wonderfully demented characterization all of which only Faulkner could have created. *Sanctuary* is an insanely good novel that was ahead of its time in its own day, and in our day blows anything Elmore Leonard or Cormac McCarthy has written way, way out of the water. If it were to come out this year, it would win every prestigious literature award there is.

It was 1929 and Bill from Oxford, Mississippi was a loser. Okay, he'd published some books. One was called *Sound and the Fury*, one was called *As I Lay Dying*, and there were a few more. But no one had ever heard of any of them. He felt like he knew what he was doing and that it was important and relevant, but he was the only one. His work was not only failing to win awards and pay his mortgage—it was failing to connect with *anybody*, to make *anyone* give half a shit. But Bill was a writer, unfortunately for him. He loved it and had no other employable skills. So he had little choice but to keep writing. But as he started to think about writing his next novel, he was feeling desperate, cynical. He thought, I'm thirty-one and about to get married, and she has kids and she used to be married to a lawyer and so is accustomed to a certain standard of living, and I'm tired of everyone calling me a fuck-up—I need a plan. In Bill's hometown, even though he had published a few things, he was known only as the pretentious wannabe writer who was always in debt, drank too much, and could not hold a job. They called him "Count No-Account." He was obscure. In 1929 in Mississippi, literary obscurity meant utter oblivion. And existential crisis meant *existential fucking crisis*. He thought, This time toss off something cheap and popular to make some fast bucks. He thought of the time years earlier when he'd found himself chatting with a prostitute in a bar in New Orleans. She'd told him about how she had once been raped with a corncob. Not only was it still possible for a writer to be truly obscure in 1929, it was also still possible for a writer to be shocking. And such utilization of a corncob was about as shocking as you could get. If Bill wrote a novel about such a thing, it would scandalize society, cause all sorts of hoopla. Which, he reasoned, would lead to some cash and notoriety. At the very least he would no longer be ignored. He cranked out the book in a couple of months, forgetting something he already knew— there are no such things as fast bucks.

His editor read the manuscript and wrote back, "Jesus, Bill, I can't publish this—we'd both be in jail." But one day the proofs showed up on Bill's doorstep. Guess he changed his mind. Didn't tell Bill that. Never explained why. Seeing it in print made Bill realize what a shitty, crass novel he had written. His pride would never allow him to publish such a thing. He took it with him on his honeymoon and rewrote it in his hotel room. It cost money to revise proofs, but he paid for the expense of doing so himself. He added layer upon layer of blackened beauty and gothic profundity, a slow-creeping swamp of desperation. When *Sanctuary* was published it did what it had been born to do: shocked everyone. Now Bill was known around town as the pretentious wannabe writer who was always in debt, drank too much, could not hold a job—and wrote that vile book with the corncob. Very quickly he was regretting *Sanctuary*. He was embarrassed by the cynicism out of which the novel was born. The cash it made was neither fast nor substantial. Another failure—he'd even failed at selling out. For the rest of his life, Bill disowned *Sanctuary*. He should not have. As with most scandals, everyone missed the point. *Sanctuary* is not cheap, commercial junk—it is the best case you'll ever find of a so-called literary writer working in genre, which back then was deplorable but nowadays is done by seemingly everyone.

Twenty years later, in 1949, they gave Bill the Nobel Prize for Literature. At the time, of all his novels, only *Sanctuary* was still in print—the desperate cash grab, the cynical misstep. Since then, his books have become synonymous with impenetrable high brow literature, tedious high school English assignments, and undergraduate academic drudgery. I recommend divorcing them from all that immediately. Read Faulkner like you would any other book you'd read just for pleasure. Begin with *Sanctuary*. What you'll find is something compelling and weighty and gorgeous and harrowing and relevant and true that will stay with you forever. ❧

Sliding Door

Nora Cameron

Martha searched the house, lifting every cushion, crouching down beneath each chair. She turned the dial on her hearing aid until it reached its highest pitch. Even at full volume, she couldn't hear the kittens' cries.

The phone rang, and she jumped. She turned the dial lower. Her daughter on the phone said, "Lose those kittens yet?"

"Not funny, Stef." The phone weighed heavily between her shoulder and her neck. "I think I did." She ran the water from the tap into the teapot on the counter and placed it on the stove.

"What do you mean? How can you lose two kittens in that tiny house?"

"I just don't know." Martha opened and then closed the kitchen cabinets, shifting every pot and pan to check beneath. "They got out of the bathroom somehow. Maybe they're outside." She moved across the living room and threw the slightness of her weight into the sliding door. It wouldn't budge.

She turned the lock. The door jerked open. The phone fell to the floor. A cold breeze crossed the room. She bent to pick up the receiver. Her arthritis-riddled hands pressed it back against her ear. She looked out at the setting sky and noticed how the amber outlines of the treetops cast long shadows on the grassy lawn. "I'm just too old," she whispered, but her daughter didn't hear. She shut the sliding door, straining her frail body as it closed.

"Be careful with your shoulder, Ma. The doctor says to rest it."

"Yes, I know." The teapot whistled, and she poured the boiling water in a mug with herbal tea and left it out to steep. Her voice shook. "I'll be fine. Don't worry. Let me get my dinner going."

"You sure?"

"I'm sure." Martha set down the receiver. Her high school picture hung beside the cradle of the phone. She ran her withered fingers over its pale glass, remembering her former lips and porcelain skin.

Her eyes stung from the tears. She went to get a tissue from the bathroom. The face reflected in the mirror scared her. Her beauty had abandoned her, leaving deep-set lines around her eyes and mouth. She ran her hands across her disappearing lips and turned away. She saw the set-up she'd created for the kittens by the bath. The newspaper lay evenly across the tile floors, the litter box sat waiting, freshly cleaned. She'd even left a catnip mouse for them to play with. But, she told herself, she couldn't take care of the kittens on her own. She couldn't seem to get it right.

She wiped her nose and threw away the tissue. She'd simply have to wait. She checked the bathtub one more time, and again, beneath the sink. Then she remembered the tea steeping by the stove.

The tea was almost cold. She swallowed it like medicine. She looked across the kitchen sink and out into the darkening yard. The tears returned as she looked past the labeled bottles neatly lined up on her windowsill.

She poured the cold tea down the drain and went into the living room. She sat down on the sofa and then pulled her wedding album out from underneath the coffee table. First, she slid the small, frayed photo out and fingered its torn edges. Her husband: navy cap and uniform, smiling out at her in the same charming way he had when he'd proposed to her. She'd been just eighteen when they'd married. She remembered feeling radiant in her white gown.

The pictures from the honeymoon while skiing in the Rockies made her thin lips smile. In one, her husband had skied down the mountain with her in his arms, and they'd collapsed into a pile at the base. Someone had snapped the photo as they'd lain there, laughing, throwing snow.

She turned the pages slowly, watching their six children grow. She laughed aloud at an old picture of her husband holding up the family rooster in his arms. She thought back to the wild impressions he would do, chasing her around the farm, crowing like a cock. She shivered. The old house felt cold.

She pulled a blanket from the couch and wrapped it round her body. Something soft and warm brushed slowly past her ankle. She leaned down and scooped the kitten up to stroke its fur. It purred. "So precious," she said, and she closed her eyes. "Stef will take good care of you. You're going to be just fine." ❧

Easy

Jim Lewis

Collaborations between visual artists and writers are often good, but seldom great. Usually, the problem is priority of one sort or another: coming up with a design and layout that's suitable for both can be difficult, and the coated paper that's best for reproductions is inhospitable to print of any length. In the absence of a good compromise, the pictures inevitably look like illustrations, or the words like captions. Moreover, it's hard to find a moment when both contributors are at their best, and in the mood to work together. Indeed, the better cases are generally not collaborations at all, but instances of a single figure working in two media simultaneously: William Blake's *Songs of Innocence and Experience* is a classic example, Michael Ondaatje's *Collected Works of Billy the Kid* a more recent one. There are exceptions. Hart Crane's *The Bridge* originally appeared in an edition that included three photographs by Walker Evans, the first he'd ever published. Robert Frank's *The Americans* came with a cranked-up introduction by Jack Kerouac, as good a piece of writing as he ever did. And then there's *Facile*, the most nearly perfect collaboration between an artist and a writer that the twentieth century has produced.

I first happened upon it in the Museum of Modern Art's library, when I was directly out of college: a thin volume produced by Man Ray and Paul Eluard, consisting of twelve photographs, mostly nudes of Eluard's wife (and Man Ray's model), Nusch—gorgeous, silky, serpentine images, around which the lines of Eluard's love poems curl like smoke from a cigarette. The whole was printed by photogravure and issued in an edition of 1200 or so; I don't know how many have survived, but WorldCat shows a hundred or so copies in American libraries, and Google's image search yields a few legible reproductions.

My experience with the book has been a love affair in itself: I saw it once and was smitten. From time to time, I'd search for a copy online, but those that surfaced were well beyond my price range, out of my league. Then one day, a few years ago, I discovered that it had been reprinted at last, in a very good facsimile edition produced by a French publisher aptly named Bibliotheque Des Introuvables. It, too, had sold out immediately, but I found a single copy online, available in a bookstore in the 5th arrondissement. I tried to order it but couldn't negotiate their peculiar and puzzling website. Still, I would be in Paris in a few months. Would it still be available? I checked every week or so, and when I landed at CDG I took a taxi directly to the store, which was hidden on a side street a few blocks from the Sorbonne. It was closed, and there was no sign to indicate when it might be open. Through the window I could make out a tiny, unkempt place, mostly given over to disheveled Situationist matériel-pamphlets, paperbacks, posters. I asked at the bakery next door and was told that the owner showed up whenever he felt like it, and no, they didn't know his phone number. It started to drizzle. I was due somewhere. It was all very *Casablanca*. I waited under a narrow eave until at last I couldn't wait any longer; and just as I was getting ready to leave the proprietor appeared, a small, round mustachioed man in his mid-fifties, who seemed puzzled that an American would travel so far to buy such a thing, but who gladly took my forty-five euros and carefully wrapped the book in a used plastic bag to protect it from the weather. And thus I carried it, carefully stored in a pocket of my suitcase for the next two weeks. Now it sits among the artists' books in my library, a crush fulfilled and never dulled; and when visiting friends ask me, as they sometimes do, what volume in my collection I prize most, I don't think about it, I turn to the shelves and reach immediately for *Facile*. ❧

Google Moon

Anna Leahy

When I google the Moon, it looks like my
milky mammogram: my dense cells implied

by lunar crust, basalt-limned, marred and pocked,
cirrus threads connect maria and duct.

If only my rotation and orbit
were as synchronous as the Moon's, half-lit

with its dark side always slipping from us,
its uppermost point longing with light-lust.

If only a googled Moon were the real
thing, if only listless chip under seal

said the whole of it, if only the few slides
chronicling all our imagined tides

eclipsed fear. Oh, to be Galileo,
to be Armstrong, to wholeheartedly know

that a picture of the Moon is not me,
nor is it the Moon's own deep, gibbous grief.

Two Cameos

Rhina P. Espaillat

I: Rita

Daughter of Spanish dancers who would train
her in their art, back when her name was still
Cansino, she was beautiful—but then,
who wasn't, in the movies? *Entertain*,
that was the mission: and to fill the bill
you needed looks to please the businessmen
who made the films. And talent—but again,
beauty came first, and glamour that could thrill
the glamour-starved at once, with the first scene.
Her name, though: would it play in Centerville?
Wouldn't the sticks, they thought, prefer some plain
English whispering *money,* for a queen?
OK, she would be *Hayworth* for the screen:
now that says *regal.* Not a word of Spain.

II: Hattie—

As in *McDaniel*—talent robed in fat,
the first Black winner of an Oscar—played
Mammy, who hovered over Vivian Leigh.
Some resented her role, her *dis* and *dat,*
the humbling of her gifts; they felt betrayed
by her portrayal of their race. But she,
who laughed at symbols, said *I'd rather be
acting the part on screen and being paid
seven hundred a day*—a royal sum—
than earning seven as a real live maid.
After she spoke on Oscar night, they sat
her in the back, where she'd been summoned from,
the Negro Section. Look how far we've come.
Who paid to get us here, and paid with what?

Charter

Adam Vines

Hundred miles out, after a night of soaking squid for swords—
no swords—everyone's packed in the berth like wasps in a comb
except me on the stern and the mate in the wheelhouse.

The sun swells on the horizon's back. The sea coughs up
bonito; flying fish launch and crash like cheap balsa gliders.
Skiing over wakes, doll-eyed speed trollers skeet fantails,

stippling contrails of bubbles. Below—black contracting
in a sweep of blue—something's balling up ballyhoo.
The mate's "starboard," the throttle pulled back hard,

and the 130's drag plate mewls its aubade, and the marlin responds
by tail-walking, shadow-jousting, then sounds, and with
every crank she comes to me too easy—a surge, a pluck of her,

then she's gone, till I reel in what she gave up, hold her hooked eye
in my palm: a bocce ball, a boiled swan egg, if anyone could be so cruel,
the dark gulf between us as wide as her pupil refusing to shrink in the light.

Floundering

Adam Vines

1.

When the tides were right
outside of Pass Christian, I would see them
heron-stalking the shallows, gigs held high

in one hand, a lantern in the other.
They were tracking beds, depressions where flounders
had ambushed a mullet or mud minnow

and had settled back down a couple yards away,
leaving nothing behind but cloudy water
and the imprints of their bodies.

2.

They bury their bodies into the dirty bottom,
waiting for prey, accepting
the coarse sand and silt

like monks accepted hair shirts,
waited for some sign of luminous grace
to hover above them

and take their hungers away.
They only expose the black pearls
of their cattywampus eyes,

one nested between the gill plate
and jagged teeth, the other lurking
at the edge of their mottled, spade-shaped head

since the eye seeped through the body
to merge with the other
when they were just fry,

condemning them to vision always fixed
upward and the terrible weight of the world.
Perhaps they don't scurry

when the giggers find them because they've conceded
the shallow graves of their bodies while in awe
of the light spreading above them,

and, perhaps, in those barbed seconds,
they're bucking in the ecstasy of what
is not their flesh rising into the impaled air.

Mediterranean

Maggie Dietz

All around us ochre cliffs
fortify the blanching sky.
A market square hums
its wares of almond, saffron
and new wine. These, Picasso's
cobbled streets, his angles
and orange trees. Everything
whole, all the wholes long ago
broken. Bread, the bombed-
out bridge of Pont du Loup.
Bright villages built into the hills.
I'd like to say the words flown
down the road, the birds I can't
pronounce, to you. Here under
an unfamiliar sun, taste with me
the sounds I cannot say. Help me
lift the hillside to my mouth.

Galilee

Maggie Dietz

Much of what there is to see is dun:
mouse and ass and sparrow, snake in sand.

But gold in wool and temple, empire.
Wine-red pomegranates in the trees.

The roof over the sea cerulean calm days,
others as drab as fish gut or ash.

The sun an eye to some, to some a coin.
Mornings, hell in the heavens warning

sailors to heed the deep beneath them.
Evening come, the wild pale horses

of the waves deliver fishers to fish,
make widows of small-fisted women,

husbands of brothers. Sabbaths the wind
won't rest; infants test their lungs.

Late sacrifices blaze on an altar where
a poor man prays, then steals the bread.

Beggars, clothed in nerves, bellow.
A girl crouches at an open window.

Above the din of lovers' grunts and
lepers' bells, the white rustling of wings.

Winter Exercises

Len Krisak

Like mortars firing shells in flaking streams,
The barrels shooting snow in arcing beams
All down the fairway now have found their range,
Laying the white stuff down in soft exchange
For greens gone brown, until the summer course,
Surrendering its flags at last, invites
Fresh, dedicated tracks. Beneath bright lights
Or in the sun, they're out in earnest force—
Parkas, sweaters, sliding from hole to hole,
Their gliding rigorous, their goal to get
Across without a spill, of course, and yet . . .
Why do the small deserters, pole by pole,
Fall back, fan out, and signal to the sky
That they need not be rescued where they lie?

Daughters of a Boardinghouse Keeper

Skye Shirley

My twin Tillie and I run like fugitives upriver,
loosen our tangled hair, lift our skirts against
the Merrimack's pull. Far past the cotton mills

and waterwheel roar we clench onto the limbs
of birches, kind strangers on our pilgrimage. The first
Sunday of each month we crouch here among mosses,

watch the new converts bathe in the river's sweat.
I saw the baptism of an old sagamore, chased
the red cardinal feather he lost in the current.

Tillie holds her white ankles into a wave,
our skin transparent like water, I can see clear
to blue veins. We weave our curls with grasses

as the chief cuts his long braids. I shushed
her crying when he called out to god,
I clung to the banks like rock-loving columbine—

In Escher's Rooms

Daniel Tobin

If I walk this fugal promenade, descending
unending stairs, chanting to myself by half-turns
my burning prayer, I would meet myself ascending
each pending step, and I—I'm one note in the scale,
trailing myself in a circuit around the rail
unfailingly, forever, in the confluence
where sense in its slow wave breaks up and down at once,
while one sitting apart stares into the ether,
out there, at what? Geese in formation? Xanadu?
The galaxy in a leaf in a drop of dew?

Sphere, sphere, let me look closer at you, mirror-globe,
hold you in my hand like my eyes' fruit, forbidden.
Bidden, I will see what I see inside each globe
doubled to infinity by redundant eyes
the size now of suns spinning their own Mobius
Narcissus—the hive of me; or, rather, my eyes
seizing what's watched escaping while they multiply,
ramify with this room, its light bulb pendulum,
lamps, tables, books, chairs, that far-off open window
I would climb through if the world would just stop bending.

What gathers along the grid to give it lift-off
softens on a latticework of atom to stone,
stone to crystal, lizard, bee, butterfly and fin,
finished and furthered in these lean tessellations
stenciled as if on air where in ribbon heat waves
helices weave invisibly envisaging birds.
This glide of geese flickering out of quilted fields
yields day and night, twin towns, a fulcrum array
of shade, the time zones of our mirror rivers
for whose selfsame mouths our boats will now wend away.

Inside the Never-Ending of this fractal cube
the viewed go on about their worldly business.
Butler, laundress, lug, lovers at one remove,
move in a clockwork of kaleidoscopic stairs
—air's quantum quandaries, its seamless fractures—
faring forward as in the compound eye of God.
Go, this tight maze beckons, through the open portal
to where the zigzag course circles to a waterfall
forever its own source. Listen: the pash and balm
of tile on ink, the deft palm palming the palmwood.

Quissett

Daniel Tobin

For Alice Kociemba

The sun on the water is an open palm.
Saw-grass stills its lances on the sand.
The boats are nodding in a heavy calm.

This scene could be an otherworldly balm.
Bright hulls trace their colors to the strand.
The sun on the water is an open palm.

The gulls themselves have given up alarm
And float suspended in windless air and
The boats are nodding in a heavy calm.

No swells, no surge, no dissonance of storm
Drumming bluntly from offing to the land:
The sun on the water is an open palm

That gestures without moving, no quest or qualm,
Just stillness insistent with a soft command.
The boats are nodding in a heavy calm

That feels like the notion inside a psalm,
Lightness lifting everything like a hand.
The sun on the water is an open palm.
The boats are nodding in a heavy calm.

"AND NOW NOTHING WILL BE RESTRAINED FROM THEM"

Genesis 11:1-9

Daniel Tobin

Life in our fortified huts brooks easy, though wind
bears down, bears up under heaven's *frumwoerc*
with its formidable *fyr* guttering earthward
from the sky-road again—a rocket's weird glare?
The pixel-hearth warms, coddled as we are,
while behind us our assay with its hoards
rudders on: the worm of us with our man-price,
word-price, and all the far *tofts* diminishing

whomever the *wealas*, whomever the "stranger."
And we, strangers to the strangers in ourselves
shadowing us through the thickets of language
like the code of some lost, primordial cousins
watching their *terminus* stride across the tundra,
fare forward with mongrel, omnivorous tongues,
adaptive, flagrant. *To enchain syllables, and to lash
the wind are equally the undertakings of pride*

Dr. Johnson wrote. Though to lash and enchain
or, as Webster mused on this làte shore, to enjoin
some intercourse with tribes, in Europe wholly unknown
keeps the dulcet prow buoyant on its course.
Kayak, totem, chipmunk, moose, tote, banjo, juke,
make their music in the "Native Grand Opera"
with *schlep, hex, hoodlum, shanty. Brogue*-speakers wear
a shodden tongue, but it skips on, and *bling*

has become *de facto*. While far off, the Monchak
slog into wastes, *chochtar*, against the current,
their one of many words for *go* before their gone.
And the Nivk with their multiple names for pairs
de-couple from the planet's itinerant train.
Come back, Pomo, with your computation by sticks,

infinite sticks in the mind, your great woven creel,
the last ten of you subtracting, *k'ali*, to none.

In Siberia the Tofa, just thirty of thousands left,
still round their lives by the moon's nomadic light,
Hunting with Dogs Month, Gathering Birchbark Month,
and ride the castrated reindeer beyond the ice to join
the Morovo where the snake they call *ground-fish*
parses to a school that aggregates, *uduma*, to a
single body, or moves, *sakoto*, the way mourners
in procession almost undulate in their grief.

Always these grim goings—how the women
keen over their bombed, their broken, *Habibi*,
and the world become suddenly unspeakable.
You can see it, now, in the shelled look of the girl
cradling her fiancé back from war, his skull
a fissure where the shrapnel shrieked its expletive;
can *hear* it in those primal stares without sound,
huddled forms in a cave by the edge of a wood—

Habibi, Oh my Beloved, Oh my Dear One.

The Passover Weddings

Atar Hadari

That Pesach we were late getting away
After last minute cleaning, clearing, burning
And only got on board just before twelve
To hear the Egged bus resume its roar
And whisk us off the gravel
Over the engine and the chattering children
To the highway and the roar down to Jerusalem.
The way through the Rift has always been scary
But it's different in daylight with the little villages
Right by the roadside and Arab boys with earthenware pots,
Goats and tents near enough between the dunes to spit into;
The other road is where you see small towns, Afula, Hadera,
Spilling their trees and trowels across the ribbon,
Small central squares filled with ears,
The same pizzerias, same bakeries, same hooded faces –
But the Arab towns are all different,
Each incomplete in a different fashion –
This one abandoned by a mosque,
This house complete except for a front door;
And the boys run back and forth across the road
Hawking vegetables, unless of course there is trouble abroad
But then you'd speed and the bus's shatterproof glass
Would justify the tinting, and you wouldn't listen
to the song that was playing over the driver's head.
But now it's dusk and the cry of muezzins
Fills the pink stone in the gardens
And we swing past the checkpoint
To the parting of the roads to Sodom
Or up the winding narrow road through hills to Jerusalem.
And we swing right through the white dirt
And follow the sound of the singing
For it seems it's prayer-call time
Even in the city with its ever divided dreaming

And the weddings are starting now
Just before dark begins a new dateline,
The last opportunity to dance
Before Passover and its regimen of un-permitted grain;
There are weddings in every town square,
Weddings in every hall and every mansion,
The girls that will not wait till thirty days are gone
Must drink from the cup before darkness
And see it smashed before the veil is raised in a whisper –
The women dancing, the boys standing in wait
Like dandelions to leap the field
And burst into the first furlong,
Girls waiting among dancing girls like stones
Surrounded by glimmering amethysts –
All fade as the moon slowly rises and the cries of the muezzins launch
   once more
Over the green and the red and the yellow lights over the prayer halls
Over the stone that's blanched white under the daily sun,
And now we are accelerating,
Hurtling through the city of a hundred gates at breakneck speed
Watching the convivial, coagulating black robed dancers
Leaping through the air of a wedding in separate men's and women's rings
And fur hats bobbing on top of the rain of upraised hands
Circling like a wolf's pelt on top of a pail of cream –
We lose speed block by block, women and children are unpacking into
   the aisle,
Lit up stores are flying by like bits of tinsel,
Tail lights on the bridge going out of town trail back like spots of blood;
And the blue in the roofs of Jerusalem
Blue as the sky to keep the evil eye away
Darkens into a sea that will engulf tomorrow,
We are in the mouth of the Central Bus Station, Jerusalem
And outside it is raining sweets while muezzins undress the moon
And children spill onto the yellow causeway throwing caution to the
   wind
And open their hands every which way to catch the un-insulated elements
And sing the latest air-wave played

Redaction of a prayer too old to mean anything but itself,
And run before the red is gone from the horizon where cars bleed
And have already begun to groan and beg to be unsealed
And honk and honk the cry of next year in Jerusalem
And take wedding party guests to where they will eat
Their first mouthful that isn't bread
And hasn't any trace of what can ever rise again.

Dinner and a Movie, Green Canyon, Utah

Michael Sowder

As in a landscape painting of the T'ang,
snow silhouettes these black-and-yellow cliffs.
Subalpine fir stand green against the white,
holding fast for a spring that won't come.

Snow silhouettes the yellow limestone cliffs
though we can see barely any of it,
as we wait for a spring that won't come,
nestled in the back of our minivan.

We see the lights of Logan far below,
parked in the gravel mouth of the canyon,
nestled in back of our new minivan
as if on that hill over Hollywood

above the California canyons.
And we're watching a movie, *Juno*.
It's not the Hollywood take on Hera, wounded,
jealous, and roughing up Hercules,

or is it? It's all about love, and we're eating tarts,
chocolate-filled, gift of the Mayan gods
(whom sanguine Mel offered up on film)
and sipping oolong with night-blooming jasmine.

Take this Mayan gift, this chocolate tart, my
little tea cake, and I'll sing Happy Birthday!
We'll sip hot oolong with night-blooming jasmine,
for it's April, when faces called flowers—

my little tea cake, Happy Birthday!
For after a dinner at *Le Nonne*
(where flowers were floating from flowerpots)
with *amatriciana, pomodora,*

a birthday dinner at *Le Nonne*,
a nice Chianti and no dessert
(after *amatriciana, pomodora*),
rather than steal into our home like thieves

tipsy with Chianti and no dessert,
tiptoeing down halls (*bye-bye*, to the sitter),
and watch a film without waking boys, like thieves,
we drove out here where beside our *Sienna*

a deer and three fawns tiptoe through the sage
(*artemesia tridentada*),
mountain nymphs outside the van. Away
they leap when lonely headlights crest a hill

never seeing Artemis draw her bow.
I worry about cops. You say, *we're legal.*
The snake eyes creep down the hill.
It's just kids—anxious for each other's tongues.

But I worry even if we're legal,
remembering high school nights in gravel lots,
teenage *joie de tongue* interrupted
by flashlights of the Alabama law.

They pass our cliff-sheltered lot, and I sing
Happy birthday, my bow-and-arrow beauty!
What flash or light of law or shooting star
could have called the hand that brought us here,

my bow-and-arrow beauty? Happy Birthday!
Among these deer and stars not even Juno
could have called the hand that brought us here—
as into a movie you'd wished you could be in,

with deer and stars, Juno and Artemis,
where subalpine fir stand green against the snow,

a Western romance you've found yourself in,
or as in a landscape painting of the T'ang.

The Accidental Stage

Sean Keck

In the inlet weeds, where fishers' lines
tie themselves across the tide, cut on rocks,
snag on buoys—I caught a shark

that dragged my bait until both squid and it lay
halfway buried in the dirty sand, and flotsam
ringed its dorsal in a scummed gray oval.

The spots across its back were brown
and at each tail thrash shivered out
like wincing eyes. My hook stuck down

beside the famous gaping mouth. From a stone
above the accidental stage, I watched it writhe
and pull against the line no longer held.

Only its milky-black marble eye
fixed my silhouette against the sky,
reflected my smallness, even as it died.

Travels in Moominvalley

Caitlin Horrocks

For years now, I've been seizing any baby shower or child's birthday as an excuse to buy the family a Moomin book. They aren't always particularly appropriate gifts. They are, as children's books go, dense and wordy, with illustrations of creatures called Moomintrolls that look like hippos with long tails and accessories—Moominmamma wears a striped apron, the Snork Maiden a gold anklet. Moomins are cute, but many of the other denizens of Moominvalley are spooky or existential—Hemulens smell like "old paper and worry," the Muskrat lies in a hammock reading a book called *The Uselessness of Everything*, and the ghostly Hattifatteners appear on dark nights at sea, white wiggly tubes with jazz hands. But still I urge these books into parents' hands, a Moomin evangelist, wanting as many people as possible to read about these wise little Scandinavian hippos.

I let people assume that these books are relics of my own childhood, that I grew up reading *A Comet in Moominland* or *Moominsummer Madness*. But I'd never heard of them until after college, when I was working at an elementary school in Finland, where Moomins are a part of the cultural fabric and a point of national pride. The author and illustrator, Tove Jansson, is a Finn who between 1945 and 1970 created Moomin chapter books, picture books, a daily comic strip, designs for Moomin dishware and shower curtains and stuffed animals. There are Japanese and British television series, and a Moomin-themed amusement park. Jansson eventually tired of her creations and turned her attention to painting and to adult literary novels. But the Moomins remain possibly Finland's most successful cultural export. I'd still never heard of them. They were just kids' books, I thought, so I didn't bother to bring myself up to speed.

I finally read *Finn Family Moomintroll* when I was given a copy as a parting gift. An early Moomin book, *Finn Family* is lighter, more playful than the later books. The adventures involve a mischievous top hat and a house overtaken with indoor jungle foliage. The writing is charming, completely satisfying to even an adult reader and durable enough to survive translation into English ("This day the spring had decided to be not poetical but simply cheerful.") The "poetical" is never forced: the August moon is described as "unbelievably big and a little frayed round the edges like a tinned apricot." There is a genuine sweetness and joy to the illustrations, the characters, the story. But there are also villains like the Groke: "She was not particularly big and didn't look dangerous either, but you felt that she was terribly evil and would wait forever."

The books are not high fantasy; it would not occur to the Moomins to battle or exile the Groke. She's just there, to be pitied and avoided and perhaps to inspire bad dreams that can be safely woken up from. Threats are never exactly vanquished in Moominvalley because threat is omnipresent, but yet not overpowering. Moominmamma is waiting with fruit juice at the end of even the strangest experiences. In *Moominland Midwinter*, the book that hooked me on the series, the young Moomin family son wakes up early in the usual winter-long hibernation. He can't rouse his family, so he ventures into a transformed and foreboding world, leaving his old life behind: "They were very small tracks, but they were resolute and pointed straight in among the trees, southwards." The book has the clever little details that seem to come so effortlessly to Jansson (a proper pre-hibernation supper is a soup tureen of pine needles), and the illustrations are alternately huggable and desolate, as Moomintroll learns to ski or stands whimpering for his mother in their darkened house. But the book is also suffused with a deep wisdom: Moomintroll starts to grow up while his family is sleeping, and greets them in spring knowing he'll never quite be able to describe who he is now.

That sense of threat and coziness, safety and adventure, is constant in the Moominhouse, in the Moominvalley, in the sea islands and forests beyond it. Jansson writes, "There are those who stay at home and there are those who go away, and it has always been so. Everyone can choose for himself, but he must choose while there is still time and never change his mind." But this doesn't actually seem true for anyone in the Moominvalley, or for the reader. The Moomins, with as cozy a home life as anyone could want, still long for adventures, going to live on a rocky island or climbing a mountain to view a looming comet. The books allow the reader to do the same thing, to see both wonders and shadows in a world so tight and tidy and hidden you could imagine discovering it under some leaves in your own backyard.

The last book in the series, *Moominvalley in November*, features almost no Moomins—just friends and acquaintances who show up in the valley, drawn by their homey memories, to find it empty. In the abandoned Moominhouse they settle anxiously to wait for the family, wondering what could have happened to them. "You've no idea what has broken loose in this valley!" one character panics. She's told: "Don't fuss, there's nothing here that's worse than we are ourselves."

This is the not the starter title I give to prospective Moomin converts—if I'd read *Moominvalley in November* as a child, rather than as an adult, I might have cried or thrown it across the room—but as I do my best to spread Moomins far and wide, I hope some of those readers start with the summer adventures, or with the comic strip treasuries, and make it all the way to the darkest, loveliest, wisest parts of Moominvalley. The journey is worth it. ❧

Exact Science

Joshua Ruffin

Lauren called last night: Damien is leaving
her, moving back to California. The way
she says "No, Josh" when I ask if he told her why
puts the conversation to bed, and I think
I understand that bitterness that comes
from knowing just things, not
the things careening under them.
I've known two-pack-a-dayers
to live past a hundred, though cancer
took my friend Taylor in the second grade
without even the token gift of remission.
Face it: nothing is an exact science.
If you asked me about love, I would say
marine cartographers map valleys
on the ocean floor by gauging the curvature
of the waves. I would tell you how in midday light
I watched the miniscule hairs around
Jennifer's nipple, faintly swaying.
I would say she tasted the same, everywhere.

Hollow

Joshua Ruffin

These days I spend
days unearthing

myself from roughage and wonder.
Peppers planted, I impose

Whoever's eyes on the budding
but only write them open

in bloom. Say
I only learned love

when a cicada tumbled
through the air slapping

blindly at my breast.
Too much thought and soon

things empty.
I press my eye

to a slat in the abandoned
smokehouse, imagine

offal grinning in the dark.
Less time ago than I touched

my last naked knee smoke
tendriled from the chimney

like unwoven cotton. My senses
perched on a woman's hip

nudge one another awake.
Summer heat, leaves skittering

across other leaves become
a controlled burn, a small jostle of silk.

Scale

Joshua Ruffin

Pluto is gone. Gone only, yes, in terms
of namesake, of what claim it stakes in indices,
its ability to whip around the pulsing core
of our existence, unaffected. Still, though,

gone—a small truth unlearned.

In a parallel universe, I'm five again: crying,
reaching into an amended sky. My
well-meaning parents say *But look, look*
how your fingers still filter the sun

and I cry harder with knowing
a celestial body is no more
graspable than a beam of light.

Gone also is the clitoris
of the 20-year-old Gambian girl,
what should be a holy-moment

scream of nerves, cut down years ago
to an empty hood of flesh her fingers orbit.
What does it say, that I bemoan this less
than a floating clod of rock and ice? That I can't help

but imagine those fingers skimming my neck
like wind, triggering a million-year genetic memory
of the gills that once fluttered there, where water
nourished the blood rushing to meet it?

What it takes to answer this: a splay of hands
to weigh real loss. To grip and knead it,
letting the chaff slip between.

The Bare Minimum of Him

Alissa Tsukakoshi

I don't pick up the phone at first. In her message, Hilary's voice is tired to the point of fragility; I call her back. She asks if I've heard about Jeff.

No.

She sighs, and I don't understand at this moment what that sigh means.

Jeff was killed.

I hear myself asking, *My* Jeff? even though I've never—during or since the three years we dated and lived together—ever referred to Jeff as *mine*.

Your Jeff.

What do you mean, killed? What do you mean, murdered? How? But where do you get an axe? *What do you mean, an axe?* No, I haven't seen the news. The same house? He never moved out? Good for him—I mean not good since he's dead—but he really loved that apartment and he didn't think he could afford to live there without me. Which neighbor? Yeah, I think I remember him. The guy sold the TV for crack money? What is this, an anti-drug commercial? Crack Kills? The funeral? I don't think anyone would want me to go.

I realize dumbly that at some point in the conversation I've walked outside. Terror wraps around me. I tell Hilary how I'm exposed in the darkness, standing on a balcony with stairs to a yard that connects to a parking lot that leads to a world where people just bludgeon people to death. We both start giggling and screaming at the same time. Go inside! I'm going, I'm going.

How are you feeling? she asks.

I say, I feel like I can't be bitter about the relationship anymore. You really can't hold a grudge against someone who's dead, let alone brutally murdered, right?

We laugh.

I don't sleep.

The news articles online all tell the same story. Jeff was supposed to meet his mother that weekend but didn't show. He missed work on Monday without calling—it wasn't like him. He wasn't there Tuesday, either. His friends flyered the neighborhood with missing person posters and infiltrated social networking sites with pleas for help. The apartment was mostly empty, initially giving the police the impression that Jeff had just taken off. Ludicrous, if you knew Jeff at all. He wasn't capable of such spontaneity.

Interviewed, his friends and co-workers describe Jeff as someone who was a nice guy. Ludicrous, if you knew Jeff at all. Or maybe just ludicrous if you were me.

I had met Jeff through Hilary. She was first in five out of six degrees of separation connecting me to him. I found him refreshing—those five degrees were huge. He'd never gone to college and his Boston accent and racial slurs were exotic to my ears raised on Bay Area political correctness.

Despite the fact that my grandparents had been in the Japanese internment camps, Jeff didn't hesitate to voice his opinion: the internment was a great idea. He argued the unnaturalness of gay marriage to my lesbian friend. He was offensive both intentionally and unintentionally, and his mix of ignorance and chutzpah was intriguing. After we moved to the suburbs, I began washing clothes in the bathtub when Jeff refused to drive into town to the Laundromat. I was car-less and for months I scrubbed away, stubborn or perhaps defeated—the feminist in me amused.

Fascinated that a person like him could exist, I stayed. I studied him like a liberal anthropologist, detached and in awe. I wanted to know what it was like to stick with something. I'd moved too often, burnt too many bridges, quit too many jobs to know stability, but I wanted to taste it. From him I would learn how to stick with something even if it meant a warped version of commitment: continuing to stay regardless. Regardless of hating him. Regardless of not being good for each other. Regardless of being miserable.

I want to call out of work, but I'm supposed to take the students to some special baseball event, and if I'm not there they won't be able to go. Besides, Jeff dying shouldn't be a big deal. He's been a nobody in my life for years.

My boss, in her bouncy curls that match her cheery personality, unknowingly asks, How are you?

I shrug. I don't know, I say. I just found out my ex-boyfriend got murdered. I tell the story and close with, And you know what the funny part is? The guy took his credit card and bought cigarettes. I mean, who just kills someone and then uses their card to buy cigarettes?

My boss stares at me, curls unbouncing. She says, I think the word you're looking for is "fucked up" not "funny."

Yeah, I say, I guess so.

I don't point out that "fucked up" is two words. I understand that she means this situation is *fuckedup*. One worded, not two.

And if things weren't *fuckedup* enough already, I get a text message telling me that the wake will be at McDonald's on Route 18.

I make so many phone calls, excited to exchange punch lines. I was going to do a drive-by and see how I was feeling, and maybe go in. Guess what? Now I can do a drive-*thru*. You know what you should order? A number five? No, a Happy Meal. You know what the good thing is? What? At least you don't have to dress up.

Hilary tells me I have to go. How many times in your life are you going to be able to have the chance to go to your axe-murdered ex-boyfriend's wake at a McDonald's?

She has a point. But despite my usual titillation with twisted situations, sliding in next to Jeff's family in the plastic booths is an experience I don't want to have.

It's the plastic that does it. The color of ketchup and mustard in plastic.

I keep going back to a copy of Jeff's missing person poster online. His brown curly hair, his smiling, yet sad, brown eyes. There's an enlarged photo of his tattoo, suggesting it might be key in identifying him should he turn up with amnesia or in pieces. When I first met Jeff the tattoo was just a bracelet of skulls around his wrist; I loved the childish façade of toughness. But Jeff had it touched up—making it ugly—shading in ominous eyes and teeth, adding a Celtic knot. The flyer omits the inside of his wrist, my favorite part that he had added—a wisp of a Gemini sign, so feminine and unexpected on him. Jeff—with his leather jacket, shaving once a week, chasing Jack Daniels with Bud Light—shamelessly sporting a horoscope symbol like a teenage girl.

I also find a copy of Jeff's obituary online. Born here. Worked there. Survived by. Loving mother. Loving father. Loving sister. Loving brother. At the end, there are details for the service. It turns out McDonald's is the name of a funeral home, NOT the fast food chain.

Oh, I lament, the disadvantages of modern day communication and abbreviated texting.

It's August on the South Shore. Hot and humid. The funeral parlor (A.K.A. Mickey D's), like all funeral homes, looks like a Southern plantation. Leaning against the white columns are blurs of people I think I recognize. The parking lot is completely full. It's extraordinary, really. So many cars. If I died, there wouldn't be that many cars. I've moved around too much, burnt too many bridges, and written off too many people for such a breadth of people to care.

Up until now I haven't been able to feel sad, but just thinking of going in causes me to cry. There's no emotional foundation—no sense of loss—just tears that fall, a panic reaction to something I will not define. I park down the street on the corner by the coffee shop we had planned on going to one day and sob hysterically.

I call the best friend and tell him I can't go in. I just can't. I can't. I can't. He offers to meet me, to walk me inside. It would mean a lot to everyone for you to be here, he says. Jeff would have wanted you to be here. It's hasn't been easy for any of us.

But it's different with me. The relationship was bad, it ended badly. If Jeff had died any other way, I wouldn't have cared at all.

You have to let all of that go now, he says.

I tell him I will see him at the funeral and say goodbye. I don't—but should—say: I can't let go of something I'm not holding on to.

The heat of the car is stifling, and I go to the gas station across the street to buy a drink. The attendant asks, Why are you crying? You're too pretty to be crying. Why are you crying? Don't cry. Life's too short. Life's too short.

I laugh at him until he continues to over-repeat himself, and the situation stops being funny. I tell him someone died, because this is much easier for the lay person to understand than, *My ex-boyfriend got axed in the head and I just wasn't at a wake that I thought was at McDonald's.*

Well, he says, all you can hope for is that they go to heaven.

This irritates me. I want to ask, What happens to the people who don't believe in heaven? What would you have them hope for? And why aren't you willing to share one laugh over the ridiculousness of irony or me or death or the misunderstandings of strangers?

I make another drive-by to a yellow house crowded by trees, with branches half hiding a plaque displaying its name. It's a historic house, over two hundred years old. It's a crime scene with caution tape and flowers left behind. There's a gravel driveway that leads to a shed. A shed where a body wrapped in tarp was hidden for the weekend until it could be driven across the state line to be left in a field. There's a separate entrance into the whole second floor of the house to a two bedroom apartment with a fireplace. The ceiling is low, the floorboards dark and wide. They don't cut down trees that big anymore to make floorboards so wide.

In the living room there used to be a piano the tenant had maxed out his credit card to buy. He would compose songs, toying with the same melody over and over while his girlfriend lay on the couch, listening and wondering why he wouldn't just chase the music dream.

The three point turn I make is full of expectations for something to happen suddenly: to close a wound, to reopen a wound, to create a wound. But nothing so poetic happens, and I drive home.

The funeral is the next day at a little white church on a green hill—again, so Southern. We are all long sleeved and suited. I stand far away from the hearse. The best friend gestures to me through the crowd.

Someone turns around and says, They want you up there. I close my eyes to pause this world I've entered where people are accepting and wanting me to be part of something I don't deserve. I've been given the place in line after the family and the best friend, and everyone else in Jeff's life more appropriate for my spot follows behind me as we walk down the aisle.

Jeff always complained about work, but his boss gives the eulogy; I'm intrigued.

They don't make guys like Jeff anymore, the boss says.

I nod my head at this. There was something old-fashioned about Jeff. Before my anthropological hypothesis, I'd been drawn to the simple ruggedness of him. A romanticized quality of blue-collared Americana.

A few months prior, Jeff's boss had offered him another position in the company. After ten years working the same machine, maybe he'd want to try something else? Jeff didn't. Apparently he'd turned down other offers over the years—I'd never known this—Jeff liked how all the work in the company funneled down to him, proud to be the sole person to oversee the stamping of the company's name on their product. Jeff's complaining is readjusted in my memory as I listen. I can see now that he did nothing but put down a life that was all he would ever have, because it was exactly what he had. He claimed he wanted more—to go to college, to quit his job—but he'd been content all along, only trying to please me in some way by saying such things as I finished up grad school and he saw my life path so different than his. Jeff would say from time to time that he didn't know what I was doing with someone like him—he knew I would leave him. I had wanted so badly to prove him wrong.

At the end of the service, we are led out of the church by the casket, by Jeff, with tragic organ music pushing us out into the heat and the smell of summer green. Some people take off their suit jackets as if to say, *it's all over now*. The black cardigan I wear stays on me. Penance perhaps.

There's a gathering at a restaurant afterwards. Jeff's mother hugs me when I walk in. I was hoping you'd be here, she says. I saw you at the church and I was going to call if you weren't. I still have your number programmed into my phone. You two had a few good years together.

I nod, embarrassed or perhaps annoyed by her touch of reverence in this care for me. I deleted Jeff's number the day of the breakup.

The family is put together and functioning. I've yet to see any of them cry. Jeff's aunt recognizes me from the time we visited her in Ohio. She had asked someone, Whatever happened to that girl Jeffrey was dating? She was smart, the aunt was told, she moved on. I smile at her story, at the fact that she feels the need to tell me on this day.

The aunt reintroduces me to Jeff's older brother. I'd met him once during the holidays. He's taller than Jeff but with the same sad brown eyes. He asks me about things I wouldn't have expected him to remember, but unlike other family members he is distant. He excuses himself, and I turn to his wife and speak to her about their baby who is no longer a baby.

One of Jeff's friends kisses my cheek and hugs me with a sense of great protection. We reintroduce ourselves; he buys me a drink. Later I see him standing at the bar playing KENO. It's enduring. It's so shameless—this desire to win the lottery regardless. Regardless of your friend dying. Regardless of having just been at the funeral. Regardless of knowing you aren't going to win. I will lean into him and try to make a joke about his failed attempt. He will shrug and mumble something as if he didn't hear me, either completely drunk or a stranger again.

I am one of the last to leave.

The family blocks the outside stairs, one of two ways to the parking lot. I give a smile and nod before beelining it towards the handicap ramp. As I turn the corner Jeff's brother catches my arm, right above my elbow—catches me the way guys do when they want your number but they've been waiting too long, and now that you're leaving the party they're forced to muster up enough courage and they end up just grabbing you. He takes me with a soft, *Hey*—.

We've rounded the corner where the rest of the family can't see us anymore, and I turn towards him and we hug and we cry. He lets out a sob and I let out a sob and we hold each other tight. He whispers in my ear, Just keep him in your heart. But I don't know what this means, because I don't want to bury Jeff in my heart when he wasn't there to begin with. I understand that his brother thinks that maybe we were happy and in love, and things just didn't work out the way things often don't, and this is why I cry. Because why would I cry over the simple acceptance of strangers? I want to be cared for, to learn how to be warm and kind so I, too, can have the type of people Jeff had in his life. But I know this won't happen for me anytime soon, because I haven't learned how to do *regardless* without things becoming twisted up somehow.

So I let go of him.

And when I drive away, Jeff's brother still hasn't moved. Still hidden on the ramp, he wipes his tears, because unlike me he has people to shelter, to not cause worry to, to not hurt any more than they are already hurting.

After the funeral I go home and sit in the corner of my room in a big shard of sunlight, AC blasting to balance the heat. I look up Jeff's favorite band online. He would chain smoke in his truck and force me to listen to Belle and Sebastian with its imitation 1970s cheesy pop sound that I hated.

I play the song that irritated me the most with its asinine title about a frog, and a stupid revelation hits me too many years too late. What once sounded fake and corny is actually catchy in a nostalgic way. And the lyrics, well, apparently it had been just a simple love song all along. But understanding the song is not my stupid revelation. My stupid revelation is that it took Jeff dying for me to finally understand the bare minimum of him.

In the weeks that follow I find myself crying at times. No reason. Hilary says it's survivor's guilt.

I think of genocide and terrorist attacks and that type of survivor's guilt. I don't know any other. What other guilt is there? I ask her. What other fucking guilt is there?

Because I don't feel guilty. I don't feel anything at all.

And whenever I find myself crying these days, I play that stupid frog song on repeat for comfort, numbing the numbness and feeling safe in the sound of familiarity, all the memories that I'd been happy to forget about. ❧

Naked with Innocence

Holly LeCraw

The Cat's Table by Michael Ondaatje (Knopf, October, 2011)

So Long, See You Tomorrow by William Maxwell (Vintage)

Eleven. Even before the noxious but useful term "tween," eleven was acknowledged as a significant age, a cusp, especially in the less sexualized, not-so-distant past. I still played with dolls, albeit self-consciously, at eleven, which is the essence of the age: one is still standing in the room of childhood, but with one's toes curled over the threshold of adult life. The vista is spread out, but one does not know exactly how to look at it, or even what one is seeing. And sometimes, one is pushed through the doorway all at once, to negotiate this new country all alone.

By the time this piece is printed, Michael Ondaatje's latest, *The Cat's Table*, will be published, and my best guess is that his readers will be relieved, secretly or otherwise, to have a book that is slightly more traditional in structure than 2008's *Divisidero*, which made a good many demands on the reader and did not offer much in the way of linearity or resolution. *The Cat's Table*, by contrast, uses a familiar trope: it is a coming-of-age story within the context of an actual journey. An eleven-year-old ("Michael"), free of parents, takes a twenty-one-day sea voyage from Ceylon to England that moves him, literally and permanently, out of childhood. By the end, he, along with two compatriots, has seen many adult mysteries up close, mysteries he spends the rest of his life unraveling, as the book swerves in the Ondaatje manner into others' lives both past and future.

This novel-cum-memoir put me in mind of Maxwell's quiet masterpiece, *So Long, See You Tomorrow*—another coming-of-age story featuring boys' friendship and an abrupt transition, illuminated by simultaneous stories of adults' baffling passions. Both have as frames the true and central events of the authors' lives: Ondaatje's removal from Ceylon; and the death of Maxwell's mother when he was (almost) eleven, when his own childhood, he later said, ended in one day. All fiction is refracted autobiography, and these books especially; still, I'd prefer not to know the degree of refraction. There's a great deal I want to remain as mysterious, and pliable, as fiction can be: Michael's two friends on board (one of whom has a sister he later marries); the Indian circus and the brave deaf girl; the ghostly dogs; the beautiful cousin, the jazz lover, the woman who carries pigeons in her pockets. And also Maxwell's unnamed narrator's friend, Cletus, and his mother's affair, and the lover's murder, and the father's suicide. And the narrator's encounter with him years later, in the crowded hall of a Chicago high school, when neither spoke.

I thought I was rather clever yoking these two books, published thirty-one years apart, and then saw what I must have remembered only subconsciously—the blurb on the cover of my copy of *So Long* (interestingly, also a galley. And also with a moody black-and-white photo on the jacket): "This is one of the great books of our age. It is the subtlest of miniatures that contains our deepest sorrows and truths and love—all caught in a clear, simple style in perfect brushstrokes"—Michael Ondaatje.

It is a particular thrill to discover two dissimilar writers who have great regard for each other. It's like finding an obscure but essential puzzle piece. Actually, I'm not sure what Maxwell thought about Ondaatje, although he might have published him during his long tenure as fiction editor of *The New Yorker*. But here's more Ondaatje on Maxwell:

> It is a learning process. It's why I'd rather read a book that is completely unlike something I could do, in the way it's written, than read a book that's very similar to my habits or style or subject. William Maxwell—I couldn't write like him if I had a gun to my head, but I love a book such as *So Long, See You Tomorrow*.[1]

But that was in 1997. And now we have these books with, at least, some surface similarities. What are these differences that Ondaatje senses? Here's a later quote, from a conversation with Colum McCann:

> McCann: I sometimes feel like a ghost on the outside of your pages. You create a kind of photograph through your writing, and I lower myself into the background of that photograph. You never tell us how to think, but you allow us to feel in the most extraordinary way.

> Ondaatje: I don't want to control the response in the scenes that I create.[2]

It's true that Ondaatje's characters, even his first-person narrator, rarely discuss their emotions, which is another way of saying he never tells us how to think. He has a remarkable ability to lay out almost pure action in poetic prose. Analysis is rare. A typical surface-skating:

> [Mr. Mazappa] seemed suddenly alone and incapable of talk, and he became my preoccupation during the meal. . .I noticed Miss Lasqueti was also regarding him, her head lowered, gazing at him through the fence of her eyelashes. At one point she even put her hand over those still fingers, but he pulled his away. No, being within the stricter confines of the Red Sea was not an easy time for those at our table.

It's a bit ominous, and anticipatory. We know the simplicity is a guise and that some of these observations will be unpacked later. And some not.

Maxwell, on the other hand, is openly full of feeling. His narrator even discusses going to his therapist. He lays out his own heartbreak and regrets, and openly parses the same in others: "There is a limit, surely, to what one can demand of one's adolescent self. And to go on feeling guilty about something that happened so long ago is hardly reasonable. I do feel guilty, even so. A little." And yet, in a strange way, Maxwell also avoids telling us how to think. Feeling, or perhaps compassion, is the great backdrop for his work, a compassion that exists also in Ondaatje although at a greater remove, and presents itself more as pure curiosity. Maxwell is able to achieve the near-impossible: a great regard for the emotions of his protagonist self (for all his characters) that does not veer into narcissism, and definitely not into sentimentality. For Ondaatje the same feat is perhaps more effortful (although, ultimately, successful)—hence the greater remove. And the admiration.

In both books, the narrators are essentially alone. One of the hallmarks of adolescence is the sense, probably some Eriksonian developmental stage or other, of feeling oneself a newly independent agent. Michael has had this feeling for some time—"Who realizes how contented feral children are?" he says, speaking of his life in Ceylon. But on board the *Oronsay*, he has lost even the supervision of distant relatives, and has only a lackadaisical chaperone, housed far away in First Class, and sometimes the Captain himself, who yells at him more than once for his death-defying escapades. Maxwell's narrator, in contrast, breaks no rules and is thrust overnight into his isolation by his mother's death and his father's grief. Sometimes "in a prison of my own making," sometimes in a more benign and bemused mood, he observes the adults around him, apparently invisible ("Once, looking over Grace's shoulder, I saw her make a grand slam in clubs when the highest trump card in her hand was the nine"), just as his counterpart, Cletus Smith, helplessly watches as his mother and his father's best friend fall in love:

"I caught Cletus looking at us."
"What do you mean?"
"As if we'd turned into strangers."
"You imagine it," she said, and kissed him.

It could be that both these narratives are photographs that the narrators have created for themselves, transforming themselves into readers so that they can re-feel, reimagine their own histories. Ondaatje's narrator says, "This was an era without benefit of photography so the journey escaped any permanent memory...Whatever we did had no possibility of permanence." And so they can be revisited years later, given new interpretations, details, even outcomes. Maxwell, in his turn, writes, "Too many conflicting emotional interests are involved for life to ever be wholly acceptable, and possibly it is the work of the storyteller to rearrange things so that they conform to this end." But more important than any self interest is the fact that these two are artists, whose first impulse is to take what they have been given and *make a thing*, a purely creative impulse that is also by definition generous, for the thing is to be shared, sometimes even with ghosts. (Asked by a therapist what he would say if he could speak to his mother, Maxwell responded, "Here are these beautiful books, that I made for you."[3])

All fiction might be refracted autobiography, but why comb through these books, or any books, looking for breadcrumbs of reality? Ondaatje seems to agree. Readers can, of course, always turn to Ondaatje's own memoir, *Running in the Family*, for clues, even though Ondaatje said of that book, "I must confess that [it]. . .is not a history but a portrait or 'gesture.'"[4] But in a conversation with the actor Willem Dafoe, he makes a declaration that, in this age of the cult of personality, is an enormous refreshment and relief:

> Dafoe: Because you jump around [in your narratives], people want to be reassured that their reaction is all right. I think so much of, even criticism, involves that impulse. And the extension of that is wanting to find out who you are, so they can interpret the work through your personality.
>
> Ondaatje: Some things are too important to share. It's not even about protecting myself, it would just be spoiling the book.

In our culture, too hurried and nervous to make the effort art requires, we have allowed ourselves to believe that reality can serve the same transformative purposes (or that we do not need transforming), and to believe that exhibitionism is the same thing as honesty. Dafoe's characterization of readers' earnest insecurities is perhaps more generous. But the point is that the embroidered, obscuring, revealing and enlarging lies of fiction are the truths we need most.

Charles Baxter remarks that *So Long* is unique "in that other people are not minor characters in the pageant of the author's life."[5] But I'd argue that, as of 2011, the same can be said of Michael Ondaatje and *The Cat's Table*. Early on, Mr. Hastie, onboard-kennel-keeper and bridge player, tells Michael and his friends ("It was easy to fool the three of us, who were naked with innocence") that men have two hearts. "'Two ways of life. We are symmetrical creatures. We are balanced in our emotions. . .' For years I believed all this." Later, speaking from adulthood, Michael says:

> I once had a friend whose heart "moved" after a traumatic incident that he

refused to recognize. It was only later, while he was being checked out by his doctor for some minor ailment, that this physical shift was discovered. And I wondered then, when he told me this, how many of us have a moved heart that shies away to a different angle, a millimeter or even less from the place where it first existed, some repositioning unknown to us. Emily. Myself. Perhaps even Cassius. How have our emotions glanced off rather than directly faced others ever since, resulting in simple unawareness or in some cases cold-blooded self-sufficiency that is damaging to us? Is this what has left us, still uncertain, at a Cat's Table, looking back, looking back, searching out those we journeyed with or were formed by, even now, at our age? ❧

---

[1] *Michael Ondaatje by Willem Dafoe, BOMB 58/Winter 1997.*

[2] *"Adventures in the Skin Trade." A conversation with Michael Ondaatje and Colum McCann at the New York Public Library in conjunction with the PEN World Voices festival 2008. http://www.colummccann.com/interviews/ondaatje.htm*

[3] *Ellen Bryant Voight, "Angel Child," in* A William Maxwell Portrait, *eds. Baxter, Collier and Hirsch. Norton: 2004.*

[4] Running in the Family, *p. 206, Vintage International edition, 1993.*

[5] *Charles Baxter, "The Breath of Life," in* A William Maxwell Portrait, ibid.

So Many Ways I've Tried to Hold You

Jennifer Tonge

The god could change

      and he moved through forms
so quickly
the man couldn't grasp him—

fish to serpent to lion to bird
            about to pull him
      from the sandy beach;

croaking toad; hippo; newt—

         and if the god slipped away
the chance would be lost
      and the desire it left
would swallow the man;

so he clung,

      nails digging into scales and hide,
teeth on a bicep, a shoulder, a flank;

raking the tender flesh
beneath the wing;

panting at the ear, the nape—

Mashallah

Jennifer Tonge

You think you'll untie the knot,
and so you get on a bus and go—

but it's not the way you thought of doing it,
all those times you imagined;

you knew where you'd go before you went
to the station, having planned it in advance.

But you think you'll untie the knot,
so you settle into your assigned seat

and pull out your water and bag of snacks.
The bus begins to move,

and you watch the names of cities
slide by your window on the fronts of other buses,

all their mysteries cradled in them.
You thought you'd like to arrive and choose,

not knowing where you'd go,
or anything about what you'd find there.

You thought you'd untie the knot
that fastens you—that odd word

that says both *fast* and *still*; how apt it is—
you thought you could breathe more easily then,

with everything up in the air.
Or you thought you could breathe more easily

than you can, that you could unfasten yourself.
Or maybe that you wanted to.

Your fingers move pumpkin seeds between the bag
and your mouth, pistachios, pieces of lokum.

You ask the woman next to you if she'd like some
and she declines, as is polite. But you're not,

so you wait a while to ask again.
Someone gave you a hard shove on a sidewalk,

into the path of an oncoming van,
so you're lucky to be here, and a little hardened.

Men trail you like capes as you walk through the streets,
refusing to enter the carpet shops

or stop at hotels that don't say *family*.
So you are hardened, a bit bitter

as you eat your treats, watching the blue charm swing
at the top of the windshield, listening

to tinny loops of Arabesque music. You declare to yourself,
casually, that if you have to hear one more,

you'll kill this nice woman,
who finally took some pistachios

and seems to be enjoying them,
who has nothing to do with any of your problems

and whom you have no intention of harming.
And then it blossoms like a night-flower,

trailing out of the radio; the first notes strum
and you don't believe but know that you are hearing it

—a song you've always loved, find weepingly exquisite,
a song not played much anymore, almost twenty years old,

used as the theme for a James Bond movie,
and you always loved them, too.

You didn't know they were considered cheesy,
or that you were supposed to see yourself

among the undressed women.
You saw yourself in his role,

outwitting and killing the enemies of the state,
driving fast cars to appointed destinations,

tossing off elegant quips as you executed
villains and master plans brilliantly.

You wanted to move through the world like that,
smoothly and glamorously, internationally,

to be cosmopolitan, Machiavellian, Mephistophelian, a sophisticate
on multiple continents, and you thought you'd do that.

Now here you are, breathing shallowly, barely at all,
because you want to hear each

perfect note and syllable of this song.
You can feel your face softening, your head drifting

to the side as if in meditation,
like a figure in a Persian miniature, or a dervish dancing,

the knot has come untied
and it is not the one you thought.

Wisteria

Catherine Parnell

She waits to remember what she forgot. When it comes to her, she feels a rush of relief, yet these little lapses in memory frighten her. She tells herself she has been busy, too busy and she is bound to let things slip. She makes a list in her head, and then promptly forgets the first item when Tom touches her arm.

"I'm thinking," she says fiercely, but she moves closer to him, and as her hip touches his, she feels exposed—as if he could tap her chest and know how she's feeling, which is a little bit in love and a little bit too old for such things. Two months ago she'd been much more rational—a clear head and a steady heart. Two months ago Tom had been *just another man.* As a lot they leave her cold, unlike the weather.

It's August, when the worst heat rises like a dry inferno. Sara feels like kindling—all twiggy and brittle—in an uncomfortably new way, as if a spark might send her and all she has ever known up in small curls of smoke. The heat and sun have broken after June and July's unseasonably cold and wet weather, and Sara's got Swiss chard, corn, cucumbers, tomatoes, and peppers in bushel baskets, all ready for the market. Black-eyed Susans, purple coneflowers, blazing star, and cardinal flowers line the perimeter of the house, but they sulk in the mid-day sun. Her hydrangeas droop. Sara knows she shouldn't water them, but they look so hot, so tired, so thirsty.

So is she. First, the day's harvest, then working all morning with Tom in her pottery studio. She would like to go down to the pond for a swim, but she remembers now—there's no time. She climbs the ridge and looks down at the glinting water at the edge of the orchard. Two Adirondack chairs sit in the shade of the willow tree. A red towel hangs from one of the chairs. Sara turns to Tom, who has followed her. "I wish I had time for a quick swim." She does; she hopes he understands she cannot.

"Make time," says Tom. He pulls back her hair, kisses her neck, gets a mouthful of potter's clay. He spits it out, spins her around and kisses her red cheeks. "All artists deserve a dunking now and then."

How confidently Tom uses the term artist. She considers herself a dabbler, a dilettante. For her there is only the pleasure of mucking in potter's clay, like mucking around on the farm. Seeds, everything comes from seeds, dirt and water. On the farm and in her studio she exercises control, rigor, and vision. Now that Tom is buying her pottery for his shop, where to her amazement it actually sells, the texture and atmosphere of her life has changed, like clay on a wheel that was supposed to be a mug but turns into a vase.

Tom tilts her head back and kisses her throat.

"Cut it out," she says, pulling away.

Tom grabs her by the waist and waltzes her across the dry grass. "You know you want to—why not?"

"Beth and the boy are coming, and then we're off to see my mother. Another time," she says, although she wishes it could be otherwise.

"Come on," he says, tugging at her shorts.

She yanks her shorts back up. Everyone—Beth, the boy, her mother, Tom—wants a piece of her. "No," she replies.

Tom frowns. "When do Beth and Devon arrive?"

Sara wrinkles her nose and sighs. "Soon." She almost wishes they weren't coming at all. She's not one of those women who love babies, and she has no idea what to do with a baby boy. Girls—she understands them, at least farm girls, of which her daughter Beth was one. But that boy? Not that there's anything wrong with him. At least she hopes not.

She knows her wires are crossed. Boys, after all, grow into men, and who knows what Tom was like as a baby? She's got all the information she needs to know what he's like as a man. Just thinking about him makes her cheeks flush. It's unseemly, she thinks, to be so taken by intimacy at her age.

Stepping slowly across the grass, she picks up the gray watering can on the steps and walks to the side of the house, passing the sundial and the upended red wagon turned morning glory planter. Tom follows her. She drops to her knees by the spigot, turning and turning the handle until the water geysers. She cups her hands, her fingers nesting a dripping puddle. The cool water runs over her wrists, sending a chill down her spine as the slick potter's clay dribbles off her arms. Tom kneels next to her and sticks his head under the faucet. His curly shoulder-length gray hair squeaks as he rubs the water through it.

Maybe she's more than a little bit in love. Although she's not entirely pleased by the thought, she admits that she never knew it could be like this, that her heart might open up, that her solitude might be so easily broken by a man. It is not an entirely welcome break. Like everything else, it has its ups and downs.

Tom flips back his hair and water flies everywhere, mixing with sun spots and flossy milkweed seeds. A monarch butterfly sits atop a purple aster. Tom scratches his gray beard, pulling out flecks of potter's clay. He sits back on the brittle grass, and Sara feels the warmth of his eyes on her. This is a heat she can endure—later. Filling the gray can, she steps lightly across the stained wood and waters the hanging plants on the verandah. When she finishes, she turns to Tom. Her lover. Her clay-dabbed, thin-ribbed grizzled lover.

"You have to go." She grabs his shirt and pulls him close. The dank smell of wet clay sticks to his freckled skin. An age spot, big and brown, covers the dendritic veins on the back of his palm. A crooked smile with a pinch of pain crosses his face.

"I don't want to."

"Tom, please."

"You're breaking my heart," he says. "At my age, that's a dangerous thing."

"Oh, get out of here. I've got things to do."

"Dismissed," he says. "But I'll be back."

Sara waits until she hears the truck, loaded with bushels of her vegetables for the market, as well as two boxes of carefully packed pottery for Tom's shop, head down the driveway before she turns around. She does have things to do. She always has things to do. First on the list is the visit to Jeanne Marie at the assisted living home where she's been for the last two years. The move to Sunnycrest had been Jeanne Marie's idea when she still had ideas.

"Here now," Jeanne Marie had said to Sara when she left the farm for the home. "It's time for both of us to move on. I am sorry to go, yes, I am, but Sara, you must find your own way. For too long you have been with me."

Sara wonders what her mother would think of Tom. Not much, she supposes. Then again, Sara has found *a way*, and that is precisely what Jeanne Marie wanted her to do. She has always done as her mother asked. Has she been following directions or her heart? Has she forgotten something? She would like to know.

When her mother moved to Sunnycrest, she deeded the farm to Sara, who felt shackled by the inheritance of the gabled house with its green shutters, white columns, and acres of farmland. Wisteria wound around the garden gate, squeezing the posts, squeezing Sara, binding her to the farm. If a time to leave had presented itself, Sara missed it. But she has no regrets. She knows no other way of life. For more years than she cares to count she worked side by side with her mother as they tended the farm, the larger fields long ago rented out to the Maartel's down the way. Steady income, steady life. A few rocks and twisted roots, to be sure, but nothing insurmountable. Jeanne Marie believed the land held life. She had been certain Sara felt the same way, and Sara had not disabused her of this notion.

Jeanne Marie had been a woman of the soil, poking her peasant hands into the dirt. They planted carrots, onions, peas, and gourds. They cared for the peach and apple orchards. Once there had been a hired hand named Reg, but he bolted when he saw Sara's flat belly take on the shape of a melon. Jeanne Marie never said a word, and for this Sara was grateful. Beth was born to the farm fatherless, but she'd fared better with men. Her husband taught at the university where Beth had been a student. And now Sara's daughter is the mother of a boy.

The boy. How impossible to call him by name. To Sara he is simply *the boy*. At six months, her daughter's son is fat and dimpled with a single curl on the top of his head. Would Jeanne Marie know boy from girl? These days she doesn't know Tuesday from New Zealand. Swinging the empty watering can Sara walks up the path. Clipping some bee balm and daisies—when had she become a woman who always had clippers on her belt loop?—Sara returns to the spigot and fills the can halfway, slips the flowers into the can and places the arrangement on the flagstone to the right of the steps. Something glitters in the raised bed next to the steps. Tom's earring. She slips the gold hoop on her pinkie so as not to lose it. Tom finds her absent-mindedness (is that all it is?) endearing. *I'll be your memory bank*, he'd said. In truth, she has grown a little indifferent to much of what should be remembered—her world has become immeasurably small and contained; she considers this one of the perks of age. But she does not want to fall prey to the cruel illness which has taken her mother's mind, and so any lapse in acuity or recall is troublesome. That Tom offers the power of his own sharp mind is nice; that she may need his help is not nice. She fingers the gold earring.

"Hurry," Sara mutters, as she moves toward the house. Talking to herself worries her, too, but she can't seem to stop. What if she goes the way Jeanne Marie has gone?

This terrifies her.

Sara bathes quickly and runs her hand through her clipped hair. She peers into the mirror and sees shades of Beth and Jeanne Marie in her own face: obstinate eyebrows, determined lips, and hues of pink on her ears and on the tip of her nose. Of the boy she sees nothing. She shakes her tube of mascara and gently applies it to her thinning eyelashes. She assesses the blue of her eyes, still crisp and sharp, not rheumy and watery like Jeanne Marie's. At fifty-seven, Sara's body is firm and supple, but her bones creak softly at night, as if age leaches in between heartbeats. Tom creaks and squeaks too, but for him these sounds signify the hard-won physical truth of a runner. When he wraps his lean body around her, Sara falls into the hope that she might be understood, that she is not to be alone forever, as she had expected. But what does she know of love for a man? Her world has been one of women. For too long, her daughter's life and Jeanne Marie's decline have taken her energy and controlled the pattern of her days. What sustained Sara? She cannot be certain, but she feels it may have been—and will continue to be—her pottery studio, where she labors over wedges of clay, tossing, throwing, drying, and firing. Her studio had been a gift from Jeanne Marie during Beth's toddler years, a nod to the solitude Sara craved, but would not ask for.

The boy, her daughter, her mother, the farm, the clay—and Tom, an unexpected surprise. Yes, Tom. She sighs. His sharp narrow shoulders, his thin crooked fingers, and his startled eyes give him the mien of an accountant in a Dickens novel, an impression blown away when he speaks. He's a bass in the university chorus, his voice a deep whiff of ash and powder, and when he spends time at the farm Sara sings with him. But her voice is chirpy and off-key. Tom often puts his hand on her throat. "Relax," he's told her. "It will come to you when you least expect it." And it does, again and again, when they are in bed together. The song is perfect in her head, an aria punctuated by bursts of doo wop bops. This music—it is a new thing. She thinks in melody and harmony. Her lists sing.

Sara checks her watch again. She slaps some pink onto her brown cheeks and returns to the porch, wearing a yellow and red cotton dress from Haiti, a gift from Tom. *When I look at you I am warm,* he'd said. *So warm.*

Even so, she is cold in the dress. Dread. She cannot bear visiting her mother, yet she cannot stay away. What if Jeanne Marie rises from the earth of buried minds? Sara cannot chance missing such a moment. But every week Jeanne Marie digs, like the farmer she was, a little deeper into her grave.

Beth's jeep rumbles up the drive and stops under the weeping willow. From her place by the porch column, Sara watches Beth's head drop back on the headrest, her arm flung across her forehead. Beth's baby was born in late winter, but only in the last month, six months after the birth of the boy, had Beth been able to make the drive to the farm. Barefoot, Sara slips across the grass and onto the gravel; she knocks lightly on Beth's window, and her daughter opens her eyes and shrugs. Peering into the backseat, Sara stares at the sleeping boy.

He is not as ugly as he was when he was born.

Beth steps out of the car. Kissing Sara, she says, "I passed Tom's truck on the way in."

"Did you now?"

"You ought to marry him."

"I can't think why I would do that." Or would she? Jeanne Marie used to say *we are not meant to be alone.* Yet there had been no man in Jeanne Marie's life, save Sara's father, dead from appendicitis before Sara's birth. This never bothered Sara. Marriage seemed so unnatural. Yet Beth pushes her toward union, afraid perhaps she will have to deal with Sara as Sara has had to deal with Jeanne Marie.

"Oh, for God's Sake, Mom," Beth kicks a pebble. "Do you have to think everything down? It will be the death of you."

"At my age there's no up," Sara replies. She smiles at Beth. "Don't worry—I won't be a burden."

Beth sighs. "Right now I'm the burden. You might have told me children are exhausting."

"It's best to find out for yourself." Sara puts her arm around Beth. "Let's walk. We have a few minutes before we leave for Sunnycrest."

Beth glances at Sara's dusty feet and shakes her head.

"Without shoes?" Beth laughs. "You'll have to clean your feet before we go. You know how Jeanne Marie hates dirty feet."

Hated, thinks Sara. Get it straight.

Beth opens the car door and lifts the sleeping child from the car seat. One of his cheeks is flushed from contact with upholstery and Beth wipes a circle of drool from his face. Sara holds out her arms, and Beth hands Devon to her. Holding the child to her chest, Sara walks to the garden, struggling to carry the hefty child for whom she feels nothing. Beth stays by her side. Purple columbine and yellow coreopsis glow in the afternoon sun; a male cardinal flaps in the birdbath. The old picnic quilt, spread out over the hammock, blends into the flush and range of color in the garden. Beth lifts the quilt and holds it to her face.

"You've been eating raspberries." Beth points to crimson stains on the quilt. Sara shrugs; she walks down the path to the thick brambles and plucks several bursting berries. Her daughter comes up behind her and Sara turns, dropping the berries, one by one, in Beth's outstretched palm.

"First of the season," Sara says. "Do you remember what Jeanne Marie used to say?"

"'Absorb Nature's blush and you'll understand love.' What sort of love did she mean?" Beth pops all the berries into her mouth.

"You tell me."

"Tom?" Beth muses.

"We should go," says Sara softly. But she doesn't move.

A thin wail fills the air, and Beth pats the baby's back. The weeping willow flicks its leaves; a branch, brought to life by a sudden hot wind, slaps the air, and Beth, startled, shields the child. A whicker breaks through the quiet afternoon, a cloud of dust appears on the dirt road out front, and a rider trots by on an old horse. Recognizing the Maartel girl, Sara waves, and the child waves in return. The horse whickers again, and they are gone. Sara walks with Beth and the now calm infant to the porch, where Beth swings the screen door open and disappears into the house. "Big house," she says to the boy. He squeals.

Sara fills an enamel basin with water from the tap. Sitting on the porch steps, she submerges her feet in the chilly water, remembering Jeanne Marie with her feet in this same basin. *You and I*, Jeanne Marie told her, *we have beautiful, strong feet*. Although Sara and Jeanne Marie—and Beth, too—own Wellingtons and garden clogs, they rarely wore them. Much easier, Jeanne Marie had often said, to work the garden when there is no separation between the soles of your feet and the rich, brown dirt. Sara rubs her little toe, marveling at its slight curve and pink nail. She does have her mother's feet, and Jeanne Marie's voice fills her head: *Our feet will take us anywhere we wish to go if we only let them.* And so they have, each step taking them further from the past and closer to the future, whatever it holds.

And what about Tom?

Beth returns and sits down next to Sara on the stoop. "Graham's been showing off the platter you made for his birthday." Devon bounces on Beth's knees, his fat little toes curling, his knees pumping. "Daddy likes Grandma's work, doesn't he?" The boy drools.

"Has he now?" Sara reaches for the boy, but he clings to his mother.

"There's been a bit of a stampede to Tom's gallery for your work."

"So I hear," she says dryly. Yet this pleases Sara. And she is grateful to Tom for his support, although she avoids the gallery, Tom's other life. She has been there, but the white walls are too white; the glass shelves holding the ceramics, wooden bowls, blown glass goblets and figures too clean; the chimes hanging from the ceiling too noisy. She does like the Tibetan prayer flags that stretch across the ceiling. They are square and contained. Blue, white, red, green, yellow—five pure lights leading to the balancing of health and harmony. These squares of fabric belong to a religion that makes sense to her. Yellow, the color signifying earth, pleases her the most. Perhaps she should ask Tom for a set of prayer flags for Jeanne Marie.

As her daughter once again steps inside the cool house, Sara rises. Flinging the basin of water into the ivy winding up the walls of the trellis attached to the porch, Sara tiptoes up the steps and onto the mat by the door. She swings her feet in the breeze. The boy cries; Jeanne Marie's old bedroom door squeaks open and Sara understands that Beth will rest for a moment as she nurses the child in Jeanne Marie's rocker. Going up to find her shoes, Sara stops outside Jeanne Marie's door; Beth looks at her mother and asks for water. As Sara heads down the stairs to the kitchen, her calf cramps. She stops, cries out, waits for the pain to pass. It does. Everything does.

Sara reaches into the cupboard for Beth's pale blue glass. She fills it with bottled water and ice, takes a swallow, and refills it. Wiping the smudge of her lips from the glass, she returns to Jeanne Marie's bedroom where the boy and Beth are drifting off.

Sara knocks gently on the doorframe and Beth raises her head. Her body and her soul seemed to hover in the cool air of Jeanne Marie's room. The boy grunts in his sleep. Sara fingers the wooden cypress cross on the wall and whispers, "We have to go." In silence, Beth holds Devon out to Sara, who takes him and holds him against her own chest. Her heart stops, puzzled, perhaps, as it always does when she holds the boy. Beth drops her shirt over her breast, and a drop of milk seeps into the fabric. Beth lifts the glass of water to her lips and drinks. Raising her face to Sara, Beth's lips glisten with water. Her lower lip trembles.

"Are you nervous about seeing Jeanne Marie?" Sara asks.

"I don't know what to expect," Beth replies.

"Some days are better than others," Sara says. "None of them are very good, though."

Driving the jeep to Sunnycrest, they pass purple loosestrife by the side of the road. Cardinal flowers dot the edge of the pond on the hill. Beth and the boy doze until Sara pulls into the parking lot and shuts off the engine. The absence of the white noise startles Beth and the boy into wakefulness. Devon, alert and curious, jiggles a plastic key chain, sucking on the bright red ring and wiggling his bare feet. He's bursting out of his plaid jumpsuit—such a plump boy. A happy cry escapes from his mouth; he flings his arms in the air, dropping the key ring on the back seat. Beth unbuckles him from the car seat and holds him up to the sky, then hitches the boy on her thin hip, his arms around her neck. Touching his plump leg, Sara thinks of Jeanne Marie's shriveled calves, alabaster and limp. Her mother no longer walks.

Sara and Beth find Jeanne Marie in the dining hall, a plastic bib around her neck, her food splattered on the table. The aide remarks that Jeanne Marie won't take her food. It's not the first time.

"Mom?" Beth looks at Sara, who nods. Jeanne Marie rocks back and forth in her chair, moaning.

Sitting down, Beth dips Jeanne Marie's spoon in mashed squash and lifts it to her grandmother's mouth, all the while telling her about acorn and butternut squash, pumpkins and gourds. Beth's a natural. Jeanne Marie searches Beth's face, a glimmer of understanding lighting her eyes. Picking up a soft paper napkin, Beth wipes the corners of Jeanne Marie's mouth; Beth speaks of berries and grapes, and Jeanne Marie's eyes widen. The aide drifts away.

What gives our lives meaning, Sara wonders, when it comes to this? The Jeanne Marie she'd loved all her life has vanished and in her place was an old, tired woman, fetid, incontinent, unable to eat or walk, and incapable of speech. Sara does not feel anger, love, or hope. Only utter exhaustion and the unpleasant certainty that this, too, would soon be a thing of the past. It may well be her future. The old terror courses through her, and she wishes Tom were by her side.

Devon sits in a high chair provided by the staff, and Beth alternates spoonfuls of squash, one for Jeanne Marie, one for Devon. The two spoons swoop between the old woman and the baby. Playfully, Beth brings the spoon to her own lips. The boy shrieks; Jeanne Marie pouts and slowly opens her mouth. Beth slips the spoonful in, and Jeanne Marie smiles. Sara closes her eyes. Before her rises the image of her mother in the kitchen, canning sweet peaches, a spoon in her hand. *Taste, my dear. So sweet.*

And then Jeanne Marie begins to weep. Food dribbles down her chin. Her feet shuffle back and forth. Devon falls silent as Jeanne Marie cries and flails. Walking to her mother's wheelchair, Sara pulls a rag doll from the carryall attached to the back of the chair. The doll's face is stained, the head plucked bald. Sara places the doll in Jeanne Marie's crooked arm. Dropping her cheek against her doll's face, Jeanne Marie rocks and croons. Devon caws. Eyes glittering, Jeanne Marie touches Devon with her hand. For an instant her eyes clear and she smiles.

"Beautiful boy," she says, and it's her voice, the voice Sara remembers, soft, wise and forgiving. Jeanne Marie pushes her rag doll at Devon, who solemnly clutches it to his chest. Yet when Sara turns to look at Jeanne Marie, her mother's face is vacant, her body still. Only her fingers move, scratching at the table as if digging a hole to plant a seed.

What comes back to Sara, what she has forgotten, is that love can live for a long time at the edges of memory. Sara lifts Devon from his chair. He drops the doll, and wraps his arms around her neck. *Oh Boy*, she thinks. *Boyo*. Devon sticks a finger in her ear and pushes off her chest like a swimmer pushing off a wall; she extends her arms and catches him as he looks at the world upside-down. He arches his back and digs his heels into Sara's chest.

This is what life does. It kicks you in the chest, resetting your internal rhythm.

Sara makes a list in her head. She lingers over each item, savoring each thought, relishing the difference between *will* and *must*.

She will crawl next to Devon in the garden and show him worms.

She will make him tomato jam and cherry cookies.

And a mug, yes, she will make him a bright blue mug.

She will wear strings of colored beads and rings on her fingers.

She will call Tom, swim naked in the pond, brown in the sun.

And she will, when her time comes, die feeling something, even if she won't remember just what it means. ཉ

poetry
ART
interviews
prose

Submit
&
Subscribe

www.
jubilat
.org

DEPARTMENT OF
ENGLISH

482 Bartlett Hall
University of Massachusetts
Amherst, MA
01003

Lights, Camera, Lesson

Stefan Merrill Block

Once, when I asked a certain novelist (who shall remain nameless) if he had ever considered writing a screenplay, he sneered. Screenplays, he said, aren't really writing; they are just written blueprints for someone else's art. I couldn't entirely agree—after all, it's hard to think of any writing more resounding than "I'm going to make him an offer he can't refuse" or "I'm mad as hell, and I'm not going to take it anymore!"—but I understood his point. A screenplay, even a great screenplay, is just a 120-page stack of guidelines, which often have only a distant relationship with the final film. The work of a screenwriter, my anonymous novelist suggested, was mostly structural, and then he went on to ridicule the tired formulas of modern screenplays, their plots' hooks and twists landing precisely on the expected page numbers, their characters' fates dictated by the algorithms that Hollywood has found most bankable. As a novelist myself, I found a certain validating pleasure in my colleague's literary snobbery, and I agreed with him that one of the great pleasures of reading and writing novels is the form's wandering space, where a narrative can unfold in idiosyncratic ways more closely resembling life's haphazard and often meandering paths.

But only, I think, to a point. The reader can faithfully follow the strange and convoluted fates of a book's characters but only if the reader implicitly trusts the writer to deliver what life usually denies us: a satisfying conclusion or revelation. And, I believe, in the attempt to deliver on this requirement, any novelist has something to learn from the sturdy architecture of even the most basic Hollywood script.

As I'm writing, trying to form the unruly mess of pages into something meaningful, trying to impose a story-shape on my own characters' wandering, there are three films that I often find myself thinking about. They are three of my favorite movies, and each offers a unique and entirely successful structure, a framework that often provides me with a scaffolding to help construct my otherwise unsound creations.

The first is Billy Wilder's *The Apartment*, a film that has become my archetype of Classical Hollywood structure. This wistful and darkly funny film follows precisely the standard shape of Hollywood romantic comedies. From the second Jack Lemmon eyes Shirley MacLaine in the office elevator, we sense exactly where the action is headed, even its outcome. Not a development is unexpected, and yet there is tremendous pleasure in the unruliness that Wilder allows to occur within that structure. In the middle of the film, Wilder surprises us by letting the structure slacken to linger in the sleepy apartment with the two stars and watch their intimacy bloom in slow, awkward, and hilarious ways. The quiet realism of these scenes is more effective because it is so surprising within the Hollywood formula. Sometimes, as *The Apartment* shows, a familiar story can be more effective for the ways it courts but also dismisses cliché.

The second film I often think of is perhaps the most obvious, with a structure so emulated that one could probably spend a lifetime screening its imitations. Orson Welles' *Citizen Kane* shatters narrative time into fragments that the film's faceless journalists attempt to piece together. The pieces may never quite fit, but the investigative structure allows Welles an astonishing freedom of movement through time and place. The structure of the film—the investigative seeking of the journalists—becomes the story, just as that same fragmentary structure expresses its fragmented subject. While no one may be able to replicate Welles' perfect marriage of subject, story, and structure, *Citizen Kane* shows how the way in which the story is told can be made inseparable from what the story is about.

And yet, the movie I think of most often when I write is Atom Egoyan's quietly heartrending 1997 masterpiece, *The Sweet Hereafter*. What is *The Sweet Hereafter* about? It depends on your angle of observation: it could be about a lawyer profiting from a tragedy, a wrathful father seeking payback for the loss of his daughter, the effects of a terrible tragedy on a small town, or a young woman's coming of age story. Unless it is really about desperate and impossible love? As in *Citizen Kane*, time is not linear in *The Sweet Hereafter*; hardly one scene follows the next in a sequential way. Egoyan moves backward and forward and sideways, through time, place and characters. And certain moments—lovers meeting in a hotel room, a girl watching a carnival—are impossible to place precisely. But here is Egoyan's extraordinary accomplishment: rather than dissolving the film into a maddeningly abstract meditation, these ellipses make the film more meaningful, and in a peculiar way, more logical. As in *Kane*, the form is indistinguishable from the story and subject; this is a movie about memory, how people understand it, deny it, transcend it. The film considers the past just as its characters do. Memories are interrupted, reinterpreted, and altered by other memories and by the still unfolding present. Perhaps the greatest achievement of this film, and the reason I return to it so often, is that somehow Egoyan's freedom with time does not at all give the characters or action a fragmented feeling. Compelled forward by emotional rather than chronological logic, while still telling a satisfying and suspenseful story, Egoyan's movie is, for me, a master class on structure. And, perhaps, an impossible blueprint to follow. But, when my own structures threaten to come tumbling down, it is inspiring and instructive to see how such an unlikely thing can stand so solidly. ❧

Your Translator, My Brunette

Amy Boutell

I have one mole on my neck, not two, and your narrator mixed up the colors of my dresses. The yellow halter dress has a print of white birds; the red satin one is trimmed with vintage crystal beads that cast shadows in the light. Summer doesn't allow me to wear the black wool shawl you mentioned with either dress. A spidery shawl, I described it once in a poem; we were in Paris, and I made you a translator, too. It's funny that we should both choose the same metaphor, the same city. I bought that yellow dress for a dollar at the Chelsea flea market. The red dress, as you suspected, cost me a pretty penny. But the salesgirl said that I wear love well, so I figured it was a worthy investment.

You're right, I do walk a certain way when wearing long dresses, holding the fabric so as not to trip. I do—I did—walk barefoot down the hallway of the hotel and dirty my feet, red polish chipped, sling off my silver heels and climb onto the fire escape to watch the sky change from day to night. The lattice casting shadows across our bodies as we sat together on the fire escape of the hotel where we stayed that second and final summer, exactly one year to the day after we met in the city that we both chose to cast as Paris.

Both dresses hung in a plastic dry-cleaning sheath in my closet for almost two years before I could stand the sight of them again. I still wear the red dress, at least try it occasionally to make sure it still fits, which it more or less does, though I've lost most of the crystal beads. The straps of the yellow halter dress no longer offer enough support. I'm a thirty-year-old 34 D and I've taken to wearing practical, comfortable bras. As for the shawl, it's become worn away by the touch of other men. But no, there have only been a few men since you.

I should tell you, by the way, that I probably owe you and your publisher a few hundred dollars. I used to make a habit of hiding your books at the bookstore. I'd take them to the bathroom and leave them there; I'd bring them to the café to use as coasters; I'd bury them behind books in the Self-Help, Metaphysics, and Women's Studies departments. I'd arrange your books on the shelf next to authors who win the prizes for which you are short-listed. I stopped going to bookstores altogether when the hardcover of your previous novel came out, the one you were working on in Paris. I could hardly read for months.

I turn to the dedication page of your book: always just to initials, never mine, of course, not even one letter of my name do I share with your wife, your editors, the other women who do your historical research. I turn to the last page of the book and learn about the entire history of a font, the two Finnish men in the eighteenth century who each claimed to create the typeface of your book. And then there's the acknowledgment page: so many primary sources, so many secondary. "Our stories never being entirely our own," as you write. When I was a little younger, I would've told myself that this was your way of acknowledging me.

I'm glad you like me as a brunette. But one thing: about the dimple on your protagonist's breast? You must've gotten that from someone else. I just spun around in the restroom at the bookstore, searching for what you might've seen or imagined. I can't help but wonder what other women grace these pages. But the Russian poet that your characters talk about in the library in Paris—I remember this all too clearly: there's no mistaking Akhmatova. *Let's leave some gaps in your biography, shall we?*

I remember sitting on the windowsill at our hotel right before my plane left in Paris, watching the cottonwood fall, listening to the summer rain, the scent of the previous night's whiskey not quite masked by my Honeysuckle perfume from L'Occitane, the trees sighing along with me as I waited—for what?—for you to tell me not to go. Or that you want to see me again in New York and continue what we started.

Did you suffer a little, too, watching me drive off in the cab to the airport, while you had one night in Paris all alone? I did wear love well. And I'll give you this: it was difficult to "shuck" you, as you write in the new novel. Both of us returning to the same city, agreeing not to exchange numbers, wandering around New York, not separated by mountain ranges or oceans or time zones, but a walk-able number of city blocks. But I didn't search for you after we left Paris, no: I did not "seek you wherever I went" after we parted. But I still found you in a signed copy of your book at a used bookstore, inscribed with a quotation that you wrote in one of your unsigned love letters to me, as if protecting yourself for posterity. *What I do is me; for that I came.* Later I'd find out that this line wasn't even yours to begin with.

What were you doing with me, exactly? I still have the pictures you took of me high up in your grandparents' townhouse on 5th Avenue, after we ran into each other on the street: rolls and rolls of pictures, in the servant's elevator with the old dial-up phone, on the rickety steps leading up to the attic where you hid as a child, and still do; on the imposing mahogany desk and the rough hard-wood floor where you made love to me surrounded by stray white papers and unfinished books. A lone splinter is probably still lodged in my thigh to this very day.

Are the pictures you took of me still burned in your mind? Do you still have the pictures, or did you rip them up like the translator did in your book? Was it too much temptation for you to "risk stepping back into that moment" with me?

Did you think of me up there in your office when you wrote your book, mixing up the colors of my dresses as if they'd fallen off my body in that very room, after you'd removed my clothing? Is this how the colors pooled onto the floor, into your imagination and onto your empty white page?

Is this where the birds from my yellow dress fled and escaped through that tiny window; is there a bird still lingering up in your attic? Do you charm him to your typewriter still? Is this what happened to your memories of me, free and birdlike, ready to take flight?

High up in the servant's attic, in the two-hundred-year-old town-house, trespassing not our faithfulness to ourselves, as you said, but our faithfulness to those who awaited us down the rickety steps, down the wrought-iron old-fashioned elevator, down the marble steps, down the concrete stoop, to life below, where the oxygen must've swiftly changed because suddenly you were able to breathe so steadily, while I stood bare-foot, silver heals in one shaking hand, trying to pull up the straps of my dress with the other, unable to find my equilibrium.

I remember looking away from you as we stood on the street in front of the townhouse—my cheeks flushed, focusing my gaze on the sign fluttering in the early morning breeze across the street at the museum. The exhibit had just left town. I wanted to disappear into quicksand, to hop ship with the traveling exhibit (the cubist's portrait of a woman's face, the surrealist's rendering of time) and sneak onto the freight train with these paintings, or into the luggage compartment of a plane, however the art departed, and leave along with the exhibit.

Did I disappear to you right then, as I got into a cab with the money you had to give me? (*Loan me*, I'd asked, immediately regretting my choice of words.) Or did some part of me seep into your memories and your imaginings, despite the ease with which you told me to leave, your readiness to hail me a cab and hand me a hundred dollar bill?

Is there a part of me within you still, lingering beneath your smoke and whiskey, like my Honeysuckle perfume, which I left you with? Is the round tin container of the scent still hidden in a desk drawer, or lost in your pocket like change? Do you take it out every now and then and smell it? I wonder if there's any part of me within you still, pressed like a leaf or a flower in a book. Because this is where I lost my footing, right there across the street from the museum. This is where I lost a part of myself, as if shedding a second skin I didn't know that I had.

Nearly six years later, sitting here at the bookstore, I find myself missing those parts of myself. I feel a little short of breath, just as I was short of breath in the cab ride down 5th Avenue. As if the eighty-three dollars in change was your last love letter to me, your first and final apology. This is how I felt when I opened up your book tonight. And after I read the passages where I recognized a part of myself—or simply imagined I did— I felt myself trying to will everything that I had shed back to me. The beads, my desire, my shame.

I don't think I'll read your new book in its entirety. A beginning, middle, and end: that was never in the spirit of those scattered days we spent together. It's all so unfinished, you used to say. But maybe one day our characters will cross paths: your translator, my brunette. Maybe they'll pass each other on the escalators at Charles de Gaulle, miss their planes, adjust their watches to account for all the time they've lost, hail a cab, and go back.

But I don't think they would recognize each other. ❧

EAST OF EDEN by John Steinbeck

Jane Roper

When I was a senior in college, a good friend of mine who had read *East of Eden* over the summer told me I *had* to read it. "It starts off a little slow," she told me in her slightly lispy, subtly Houston-drawly way, "but after that it reads like a *soap opera!*"

Ambitiously, I checked the 600-page book out of the college library, thinking I'd read it in my spare time. But between my course load, my part-time job in the dining hall, my boyfriend (who is now my husband), and—don't laugh—my a cappella group rehearsals and shows (oh, fine, laugh) I didn't make much headway. The beginning was, as my friend had warned, a little slow, and slogging was the last thing I wanted to do in my limited leisure time. After a day of dishing out lasagna on the cafeteria line and poring over pages of Foucault, Freud, and Lévi-Strauss, watching Beavis and Butthead in the dorm common room was far more appealing. So back to the library it went.

Fifteen years later, *East of Eden* was the book discussion selection for a YMCA camp on Lake Winnipesaukee where I spend a week every August with my family. So I gave it another shot. And in spite of a nearly full-time day job, four-year-old twins, a writing career—although, sadly, no a cappella group—I was able to squeeze it in.

And my friend was right: *East of Eden* is every bit as addictive as a soap opera once it gets going. Unlike a soap opera, however, it is exquisitely written: every sentence simultaneously advances and deepens the story. The characters, while they sometimes feel like "types" rather than individuals, are nonetheless compelling and sympathetic. Everything that happens in the book feels like destiny, as opposed to authorial puppeteering.

But *Eden* is more than just a literary page-turner. In fact, it's so many things at once, so ambitious an undertaking, hearing it described makes it sound like it couldn't possibly hold together: It's the saga of not one, but two families; an exploration of a good and evil; a history of California, and to some degree, America at the turn of the twentieth century; a love story; a tragedy.

More than anything, though, *East of Eden* is a biblical allegory—a loose retelling of the stories of Adam and Eve, and Cain and Abel. Adam Trask, the book's central character, "falls" for the malicious but alluring Cathy, who is equal parts Eve and Serpent. He favors his "good" son, Aron (a stand-in for Abel), over the darker and more turbulent Caleb (Cain).

Steinbeck makes all of these parallels overt—when you call your book *East of Eden* and name your main character Adam, you're clearly not going for subtlety—and at one point there is even an in-depth discussion of the Cain and Abel verses in Genesis between Adam and his servant, Lee. At times I felt as if I was reading a book that was inside out—all the seams and darts visible. And yet, as is the case with an *haute couture* jacket, it works.

I couldn't help imagining how the book might have been received in the average writing workshop: *"It's not subtle enough! The symbolism is too obvious! The author is too present! Show, don't tell!"* And if Steinbeck had listened, what a far less powerful book it would have been—smug and self-satisfied instead of bold and insightful about the ways people conform to or reject archetypal roles in their own life stories.

And how much less original a work it would be, too. In fact, Steinbeck doubted that the book would ever attain the popularity of *The Grapes of Wrath* (published thirteen years earlier) on account of its unconventionality. He said of *Eden* (as quoted in the introduction to the Penguin Twentieth-Century Classics 1992 edition, by David Wyatt), "I don't see how it can be popular because I am inventing method and form and tone and context."

But he also saw *East of Eden* as the opus he'd been working up to all of his writing life: "I've been practicing for a book for thirty-five years," Steinbeck wrote in his diaries in 1949, "and this is it." Of it he also wrote, "It is the first book," and "There is only one book to a man" (as quoted by Wyatt, p. vii).

Reading these words, I am both awestruck and comforted. Imagine having so much confidence in one's idea and abilities that one can honestly say *this is it*. This is the book I was born to write, and everything else was just prelude. (I wonder: did he sense this even as he was writing his earlier books, or was it an observation made in hindsight?)

And at the same time: Phew! I love the idea of framing everything I'm writing now as mere apprenticeship. I know that my recently published debut novel (named, coincidentally, *Eden Lake*), while a decent freshman effort, is far from great. The next book will, I hope, be a little better. But someday, maybe, I'll write my "one book." And if it's even a fraction as masterful as *East of Eden*, I'll die a very satisfied writer. ❧

Notebook of Answers

Kaveh Bassiri

GIRL: African Moslem, early teens.

BOY: African Moslem, early teens.

In a room where questions line up, a large table, its flat plane the color of hummus, rises up to the brick back wall. If you stay long enough, you can imagine it shrinking to hold its guests sitting for dinner, the scent of lamb hiding in the grains, the eye of the pen tracking letters, the orders that haven't been named. By its leg sits an ashcan filled with water, slowly releasing a shadow across the floor. On the right side of the table stands a bottle, the label hidden behind a pink and magenta plastic flower arrangement. Behind and above the table is a large window onto the rampart, closing in this dark room. Each day, the window opens to a different light, as if we are processing a photo, hanging the negative to dry. A single metal chair, with its rusted back facing you, waits for a BOY or a GIRL, whose names are collected from the alphabet of the clouds. To the left, there is a hill of sands from a settlement of stones caught by a postcard.

There are pauses at each space in the monologues as if the speakers receive questions. You can wait in the silences, rest at a door for the knock of answers, or follow as they run after those who call them.

Scene 1

(Light. A single bulb, with a metal turban, polishes the table with the color of well water. The window is black. The GIRL sits at the table; her green "tobe" protects her head and her shoulder. You watch her back as it drops and rises, taking in the weight of the room. Pictures, passed to the GIRL, skitter out from a crack between the table and window.)

GIRL
(A picture slides toward her. She looks.)
No, that's my sister.

On the other side of the hills, where the sun gets up.

I don't remember.

(Another picture rushes toward her. She looks.)
That's not my house. We have walls. I have a fig tree.

(Looks again at the picture.)
My sister and three brothers.

No.

(Another picture)
That's grandpa's. We live next to him. His house is in the middle. It's the biggest. We always wanted to play there, but we weren't allowed.

Let me go.

(Points to the picture.)
Dad gave me that. I wanted a red one, but it's pink.

Please. Yes. Yes, sir.

There were cows, goats, chickens. We had two donkeys.

We were in the next town.

I don't know why.

I bought potatoes and beans.

No, we don't go there.

Yes.

There—

Scene 2
(Light. The window is gray, the flower arrangement changed to red. The BOY is sitting at the table. Outside, the wind opens and shuts a flag. Through out this scene, we hear intermittent knocking, arrivals, salutations, farewells, the bolting and unbolting of the door. Do you recognize the one who is sitting next to you?)

BOY

There were horses and camels everywhere. Big cars. They were wearing green and tan jackets.

No. They are Moslem.

Yes.

We were afraid. I had never seen those flying blades come so close.

Yes, I think so.

Ant... Anton... Antonov. I don't know.

They said... They said, "Get up. So we can see you." He was five years old.

I could see him. His gun was shaking. He was holding it like a sparrow.

Oh, no, that's not true.

Maybe, I don't remember.

Yes.

They said, "Run. You don't belong."

No. Our Islam is good. We pray all the time.

I don't understand your question.

Yes, I can count. I can do multiplication and division.

The Imam was running. The chickens were screaming, their wings beating, jumping up. Everyone was running. They wanted to fly. I wish I knew how to fly.

No, I didn't.

They call us blacks. But we're—

I know that.

What do you mean?

She was calling, "Fatima, Fatima, Fatima!"

Yes.

I want my mother.

Oh, please. Do you know where she is?

Yes. I'll try.

He was not white.

They took everything: the window, the pictures, the carpets from the mosque.

No, we wanted a real soccer ball.

That's not it.

Dad says it is because they're looking for oil.

I don't know.

What is the word for it?

It all burns. Very fast. We were hiding in the smoke. The air was greasy.

I wanted to go to the outhouse.

They were cooking and eating our cows and chickens. I could hear the laughter, strong as the tractors.

I wanted to, but I couldn't. I couldn't move.

Imam said, "It's a day where men will be like moths scattered about and the mountains will be like carded wool."

Scene 3

(Light. The window is white, the flowers blue. The GIRL is held down by the punctuations, trussed to the chair by ropes taught to protect pronouns: he, his, you, herself. Throughout the scene, she quietly tries to free herself, while the sound of rain, drilling outside the door, slowly gets louder.)

GIRL
No, that was later. It was Muharam.

We had porridge. The school was closed. We were afraid they would come back.

No, I'm telling you, I wasn't hungry.

I was getting water from the well. But I didn't want to.

It was noon. I could hear the call for prayers. I told dad, it'll be okay.

Because I'm the youngest, I think.

Yes, five times.

Please sir.

No. Please don't.

They came in green cars. They had small horses on their pockets.

No one was there. They were in the mosque. There was a funeral for the Imam.

No, I don't want to.

My sister says it'll never open again.

Don't.

They were waiting. They saw me. I wanted to hide. But there was only the desert.

Yes.

They pushed the tobe into my mouth. I couldn't say anything.

Yes.

They pressed my wrists against the dirt. I tried to open my eyes.

Yes. YES.

My dad said it is because we're different.

No, I don't.

No one came to visit. I was waiting in the outhouse. Imam says it is like "a man who kindled a fire, and when it lit all around them, God took away their light, and left them in darkness."

No, that was later.

They were gone. I was naked. What were they going to do with my clothes?

Yes.

He was ashamed. I was afraid.

No, that's not it. *(Pause.)* I don't like horses.

Okay.

Orange Fanta.

Yes. I'll try.

He had brown loafers. One of them was torn. He was bleeding.

My head was down. I could see.

Yes, better.

They said, "You are Tora Bora."

Yes.

I don't know why.

They said, "You are the daughter of a rebel, you saw them, you saw-the-might."

No, that was later.

Yes, but I wasn't . . . I'm not . . . bad.

Yes, I study Arabic.

But, I don't know.

Scene 4
(Light. The flowers turn yellow against the window, a mirror reflecting the BOY and you in the room. The heat is rising outside. As the BOY speaks, millet seeds begin to pour on top of the hill of sand. You can hear the heartbeat of the hourglass.)

BOY
I haven't seen her. My sister ran away. She wouldn't look me in the eye, just stared at the wall.

Yes, Abdullah is my friend. He is strong. He has big hands. He is smart.

The wind was heavy. There was dust in the trees. I couldn't see or hear. But he saw me.

No, that's not true. He wasn't living with us.

I don't understand.

Yes. He had nowhere to go.

No, I'm telling you that's not true.

They were standing at checkpoints. We had to go up the hill. There were the birds following.

I heard them say, "We kill the blacks, even our cattle if they have black calves."

Hasan couldn't sleep all night. Someone had to stay up and watch, keep him quiet.

No.

They're like dried figs.

Yes.

Abdullah carried Hasan. We rode on a donkey. But it was too weak. We left it to the road and walked the rest of the way.

He was supposed to meet someone, I think.

I wanted to cry, but I'm older. I couldn't.

I don't understand. I don't know what you want.

I had diarrhea for days. But, I had . . . we had nothing to eat.

He must be angry with us. But I don't know why.

YES, I wanted to.

Hasan was too weak. I told him he couldn't.

We only had time to cover him with sand and grass. It was very hot. There was nobody else but the flies and the red ants. We couldn't wash him.

No, I don't.

Why do they have to kill the calves? They are very expensive.

Scene 5

(Light. The mirror is a window reflecting the room. A second mirror behind you has opened the rooms to each other. The table and chair in the other rooms are expecting their guests, their audience. The GIRL on the chair is still. The smell of cooked sorghum and millet fills the space between the words. The flowers, the color of milk.)

GIRL
Yes, please.

The earth is hard here. Where is the fig tree?

No, I don't know anyone.

There are no letters, no phone.

Yes. Some sorghum and millet.

I like okra.

It's cold at night. Look, these sores on my back are from the worms.

No, we can't go to the mosque.

No. We need wood.

No.

We need fire.

(The cement floor slowly glows red. The GIRL turns around and stares through the door behind you. Her lungs a candle.)

END OF SCENES ❧

NOON

A LITERARY ANNUAL

1324 LEXINGTON AVENUE PMB 298 NEW YORK NY 10128

EDITION PRICE $12 DOMESTIC $17 FOREIGN

Charcoal for Locust

D. Gatling Price

At university, she was going blind at reading. She mulled under her curriculum. Spent hours falling asleep at small assiduous desks. She recitaled lumbering sheaves. She made callused fingers. The weekday nights were empty cafeterias. Chewing became a distraction. On repeating Mondays, she received him in swollen letters. She waited to open them to know where he was in the world. Minarets and I.E.Ds. The ark in the instruments she handled became fastidious. Octaves beat like a million of wings. The faculty stood up and pointed fingers at her. It went on to the last refrain. Five months to a swath. Three years to a cut. Holidays and parades.

On the phone she was:

"I miss you more."

"It's only years."

"We'll have every day."

"The rest of . . ."

"I'll hold to it."

"I love you."

"No, more."

When she came home, old records. He was drinking grain alcohol let from peaches. She smoked opium, eyes black on the ceiling. Seventeen year Locusts had come up outside. Oak branches let on the shade of an ocean moving with the weight of tiny burdens. She talked in maxims. Their clothes neatly floored. The room was brown and red. No lights turned on at evening made all the noises outside high pitched and slow. She rolled onto her chest and stared across at him standing. He stretched his skin to a hide. Four years had gone by. They hadn't to eat. He walked across the room and up the bed running his hand from her outstretched heel. She put her mouth to his thigh. Picture frames on the dresser and bedside were flat down. The hours got away. Days upon days. Train cars went north south outside of earshot covered like billboards by a million of wings. Born of the naked soil, they decided right then.

The air outside was thick with bodies. When they got in the car, it all followed them in. She grinned with her mouth closed. He would buy the ring or crackerjacks.

Everything was getting engaged.

She said, "Tradition."

She repeated it.

And "Vows."

He grinned; backing the car down the sounds of the fishhook gravel drive, there was no telling what was stone.

The getting home was slow.

They stopped for every light twice.

He dropped her off.

She went half inside the screen door. The breeze picked up her hair from the east. He held her eyes in the porch light.

She wasn't going back. She went inside.

He would find out the next morning gathering the paper from the front lawn. A plague it would turn out. Land subsidence is what they would call it. "And the earth will swallow you whole." Had been said. It was an article that came off in his hands. It went:

> Underground cavities that collapse can often have profound effect on surfaces, structures, and on any intervening features such as doormats, bathtubs, living rooms, dental work, fingernails, paint brush, hair, expectations, etc. The size of the amity, its depth beneath the surface, and nature of the happenstance in the intervening layers are important influences in the extent of breakdown. The most destructive events tend to occur where the chest cavity is only a few feet or a few tens of feet below the skin, regardless of other factors, a heart. Figure 1, shows the relationship of a coalmine void to a potential supernatural event. The zone of maximum subsistence occurs directly above the collapsed opening. The damage does not end there, however, but extends outward to encompass a much larger area at the face, as shown by the profile of a life in figure 2. A man in figure 3.

He sought out every word she ever said in the wallet-sized image next to the last line. When the phone rang over the whine of collecting wings outside:

"We hoped you might be there. We have. . .well, news."

"The house."

"A retreat mine."

"No one . . .

Out alive."

"No one."

"Years and years."

"Cicadas."

"The thousands of holes."

"She was . . ."

"They all inside."

"I'm sorry."

Then
"If there's anything."

There was. Cut short in the slurry and overburden of the land. She was now under it all. The water drained of the reservoir. The act of drinking the tap out of local wells became putrid. The vacancy was all over the TV. It was an ongoing investigation. The remains would never be recovered. Committed in grout. It pulled his limbs tight and bruised his veins. He never understood. He never identified anything. There wasn't a funeral. There was a service. The man at the pulpit said, "That's the speed of things." The tragic man wondered if he hadn't listened right.

For days, all he did was step on a million of wings. Staring eyes. Places her hands had been. Polaroids and wallet sized, he took it all out on the porch and built a box for heat.

As it burned, he followed the carbon feathers through the holes of the porch. He wouldn't go outside. He wouldn't for months. The ash and dust. In it all, he sang something under his breath, between his teeth. He watched her out into the cicadas. The sounds made him all apart. ❧

IN A STRANGE ROOM by Damon Galgut

Dave King

Minimalism can be the trick gun in the artist's arsenal, sometimes hitting its target dead on, often fizzling in a spiral of sparks and a tiny flag that reads BANG. Limitation, austerity, restraint: these all make the practitioner seem mysterious and discerning while warding off a multitude of overwriting sins; but to the reader such methods can feel a little arch, like a code whose solution is just a simple algorithm, rather than a sequence involving narrative drive, reader identification and plain bubbling emotion. Which is what I like about Damon Galgut's terrific *In a Strange Room*: its methods (austere, minimalist, intentionally limited) seem much more avant than its goals. Here's a book that proposes striking experiments in conventional realism, yet remains, in the end, a deeply realist work of fiction.

I must have missed the issues of *The Paris Review* where these pieces appeared as three linked novellas, and I'd never heard of Damon Galgut until *In a Strange Room* was shortlisted for the 2010 Man Booker. Then I read a review, and still I might have passed the book by, but the reviewer noted a ribbon of homoeroticism, and that hooked me. I read it in days, my initial coolness mounting to admiration, then awe. More on that soon, but since this column's entitled "Recommendations," here goes: *This is a remarkably original book. It's brainy and cool and consistently stimulating, and it takes serious chances. In the end, it's profoundly moving, too.*

(In fact, *In a Strange Room* was the second of Damon Galgut's works to hit the Man Booker shortlist; a previous novel, *The Good Doctor*, was a 2003 finalist. Galgut has published seven volumes of fiction and four plays, and his relative obscurity in the U.S. is entirely our loss.)

Subtitled "Three Journeys," *In a Strange Room* applies a nearly identical structure to three emotionally different encounters. In each case, the protagonist sets out from Cape Town and engages some fellow traveler before returning home. But though the visited lands are described with pristine straightforwardness and the details of passage meticulously noted, Galgut's focus is abstractly restrained. We're told little, for instance, about the hero's life at home, about his childhood or family or his preoccupations when not on the road. Such details emerge scantly and only as needed, and this, combined with the impeccable descriptions, reinforces the view of travel as a heightened but dislocated sensate experience. A mirror, in some ways, of ordinary life, but separate from it.

If Galgut's travelogues offer handsome background scrims, the book's heart lies in its human interactions. (Though plenty of subsidiary characters appear, a single relationship is the focus of each novella.) Ambitiously imagined and elegantly executed, the primary interactions are so smartly connected that at its end, *In a Strange Room* is indubitably a single work, as opposed to the trio of variations it seems at the beginning. And though Galgut's formal decisions *are* austere, the book's narrative sweep is anything but; by its final pages, his protagonist has become a character of stunning nuance and depth. The three travels, apparently alike at first glance, have been differentiated by unexpectedly inventive action, including suspense, and what once seemed the very model of detached prose has managed somehow to reduce the reader to tears. It's an astonishingly sure job.

Galgut's clarity of purpose is evident in the titles he gives his three novellas. The first, "The Follower," is the best tale of passive-aggressive friendship I've ever read, made particularly stark by the narrator's impotence in the company of a demanding, inscrutable hiking partner. The second, entitled "The Lover," takes us out of the wilderness and into a realm of visas, graft and political sovereignty. This is the gay story, in which a leisurely tourist itinerary bends increasingly toward a changeable, uncertain love interest, and though in my opinion "The Lover" stands least fully on its own, it forms a solid bridge to the third tale, called "The Guardian."

"The Guardian" is in some ways a synthesis of the earlier stories, but with a significant twist, for whereas those pieces focused on strangers encountered along the way, here the companion is a beloved but troubled friend, and the journey—to India—is one ostensibly of healing. Now, in a narrative of heartbreaking disintegration, the same forces of aggression and desire are in play, but heightened by time and intimacy. The struggle for power between people who know each other well; the shifting responsibilities of loving and being loved; and the ultimate unknowability of another being, no matter how close: all are foreordained by the book's earlier sections.

I mentioned an initial coolness, which relates to the author's modern or postmodern formal choices. For one thing, the book *looks* minimalist: page breaks between paragraphs and many one-line, even one-word, paragraphs. The only punctuation is the period, and the action occurs in the present tense, all of which contributes an aestheticized formal fussiness that would be annoying if the content were less compelling.

A more potent and interesting invention, though, involves the protagonist's identity, which expands and contracts as if activated by a bellows. The opening paragraphs refer only to "he," and when, at the bottom of the page, the narrator steps forward as "I," it seems clear that there's a storyteller and protagonist subject. But gradually, over the course of "The Follower," the first and third person commingle, sometimes even in a single sentence, as here: 'So in the first few days I become aware of certain differences between them.' And when, on page twenty, the protagonist introduces himself, he says, 'I'm Damon,' suggesting the author's own involvement—or faux- or wish-involvement—in the plot. It's a strategy that slyly courts reader identification, and it pays off in "The Guardian," with its veins of intimacy, love and sorrow; the protagonist's complexity is almost cubist by the end. If travel is a mirror, Galgut seems to be saying, then fiction, of course, is some kind of mirror too. ح

The Turns They Have Taken from BYE-BYE LAND

Christian Barter

One must have deeper motives and judge everything accordingly,
but go on talking like an ordinary person.
—Pascal

Senator, the Supreme Court has not addressed that decision
straight on. But in Hamdi, the Court said the United States could
detain an American citizen, here in this country, for the duration of
the hostilities, without filing charges.
—Alberto Gonzales

A sizeless city, a crystal blooming
in a crevice of the cave floor, toy-like tiny,
near and distant—clarified by distance
to something clean enough to touch
like a battle cleansed by history,
its plains and craters bright and sharp—

Brilliant city: pinholes in a sky
that lets light through from a fire blazing beyond it—

Looking back from the Verrazano,
or over from the BQE or a dock in Red Hook,
Manhattan like a constellation
unable to break free of the earth.

Unable to break free of the earth,
taking the turns they have always taken,
they cross Fifth Avenue, cross the Brooklyn,
more absolute than ever,[1]
Manhattan like a consolation
for the caged dark of these endless crossings
for the turns they have taken and cannot take back,

Manhattan like a compensation
of twenty bucks in trinkets, for the night.

---

[1] *"and this truth, now proved, / That made me exile in her streets, stood me / More absolute*
than ever." Hart Crane, The Bridge.

It was comedy. Pure comedy.
When Frickie went up to that chick with the shaved head?
And was like, "Can I touch it?"
And she wheels around like she's in the fucking Exorcist
and says, "I have cancer, you piece of shit"?

And they go on talking like ordinary people

In the halls of high buildings, in the backs of cabs,
in the giant foyer of the Natural History Museum,
around dem bones, dem dry bones,[2]
in the Lysol-armored seats of cineplexes,
at The Statue with its bronzed broken shackles,
standing watch for the next hull-load,
in under those little tarp-things where the doormen
stand watch against an army of the homeless

In the hush of the MoMA, broken only
by the buzzing of incoming texts

wherever the just exchange their messages[3]

They dress up in suits and slick their hair
and talk out of boxes hanging on the walls

that let light through from a fire blazing beyond them.

---

[2] *"Dem Dry Bones," a famous spiritual poem and song.*

[3] *W.H. Auden, "September 1, 1939."*

Oh yah, they walkin' around like Professor Dumbledorf
with their hands behind their backs, face all scrunched up
like somebody just pass gas and they the one
been put in charge of the Central Committee
on Finding Out Whose Butt It Was.
Oh, they got all this shit here figured *right* out.
It's all "this period" and "that period,"
and the "use" of this, and how "bold" somebody was.
"That was *bold*," they say, going after the chin.
"That was a *bold use* of color." "What a *bold line!*"
I tell you what—if drawing a line on some paper?
Is *bold?* Then me going back home to the Bronx
must be a blatant act a heroism.
This chest right here ought to look like Tommy Frank.
Bold. You'd think with all these geniuses
this wouldn't be a such a fucked up place to live.
I'd like to round up all these geniuses
and say, Now how come all this killing going on?
And how come all these kids come home from school
and they don't know nothing? They can't *add,*
they can't read a *book.* And why is it the *case*
my mama work thirty years up in that *home*
changing old men's diapers and if *she* go
up to see the doctor, they all
Ma'am, what kinda insurance has you got?
Now if you could all just pull yourselves away
from these here soup cans—Oh, yah! Soup cans is *big.*
And they *bold,* too, if everybody right.
They got a room with nothing but a toilet in it!
All this carrying on. And what's it for?
You got a stain. Right there.
No, let me get it. These white uniforms—
you can't get within a hundred feet of food, hon.

*What about a case here, an American citizen,
in the United States?* [4]

---

[4] *Senator Patrick Leahy questioning Alberto Gonzales about U.S. use of torture; 6
January, 2005.*

The elephant in the room is *brontosaurus*,
his neck stacked high
to the inbred royalty of his tiny head,
his ribcage showing through to more of themselves:

they who walk among the bones for hours
the way they walked in the baths of Rome,
in the streets of Athens, Byzantium—
a step towards peace—
a step towards reason—
a step away from war—[5]

Protoceratops, allosaurus,
stripped down by dust to just their armor,
the brutal shields and horns and teeth
the only thing left to say what they once were

like broken statues or boxes of old letters—

Your Reverence writes me that you would like to know
whether the Negroes who are sent to your parts
have been legally captured[6]

What killed them, Mommy?

Meteors.

---

[5] *"But it is an important first step—a step towards peace—a step towards reason—a step*
away from war." Kennedy, on the Nuclear Test Ban Treaty of 1963.

[6] *Brother Luis Brandaon, March 12,1610: "To this I reply that I think your Reverence*
should have no scruples on this point, because this is a matter which has been questioned
by the Board of Conscience in Lisbon, and all its members are learned and conscientious
men. Nor did the bishops who were in Sao Thome, Cape Verde and here in Loando—all
learned and virtuous men—find fault with it."

And the city breathed.
It heaved and sighed.
The groans of lifting heavy stones.
It squeaked and clanged.
Whole villages slid by on rails.
The frantic boredom of car horns.
The war-whoop of sirens coming down from far-off hills.
All of it like a silence.
Like a stutter.
A disturbed man shouting the same words over and over.
What do you think it means, doc?
Well, I don't know.
Sometimes these things don't really MEAN anything.
Metal on metal, fumes exploding in chambers.
Air brakes crashing like waves
sent in by a storm that hit Haiti days ago.

Dude, you made it. Sweet. You need a beer.
This is Mauriana, by the way.
And *this* is the art salon. Check it out.
Oh, man, have you even *heard* the 10,000 Maniacs
in years? I love it. Turn it up!
It's like they're good all over again.
This guy does installation pieces.
It's a faucet coming out of the water. Right?
And this thing here—
well, I guess I don't know *what* this is.
Some kind of po-mo parakeet. I love it.

Dude, what the fuck? You need another tall boy?
Look at this thing. It's a grouchy Buddha-dude
squatting down a teeter-totter.
"Pudgy Wins." I love it. What do you think?

I think continually of those who were truly great.
Who, from the womb, remembered the soul's history [7]

Dude, check *this* out: his afro's made of pennies.
It's, like, an ironic version of emancipation—
an afro made of Lincolns.
And look at his expression—he's like,
"Dude, what the fuck?"

---

[7] *Stephen Spender, "The Truly Great."*

It is dark along the streets, bright high in the buildings.
Bright past the buildings where Manhattan stands
in a robe of light. Its light is like an argument,
an argument it makes with each man looking,
an argument that will not be talked down.

Senator, the Supreme Court
has not addressed that question straight on [8]

The dark is local. The light takes over
the farther one looks away. The light is public.
It insists on life. On hope.
The light would never pull the plug.
The light cares nothing for misery.
The light only acknowledges positive feedback.
The light is a conversation at a party
where every private fear is polluted with confidence.

---

[8] *"Senator, the Supreme Court has not addressed that decision straight on. But in Hamdi,*
the court said the United States could detain an American citizen, here in this country, for
the duration of the hostilities, without filing charges." Albert Gonzales, op cit Gonzales
testimony 6 January 2005.

It's good to be with you, Dana. What's happened so far
is they've charged him with a class C felony
for having the gun illegally, which carries
a minimum sentence of three and a half years.
The fact that it went off in his pocket may lengthen that.

But I think what everyone wants to know, here, Dana,
is why would Plaxico have a gun to begin with?
He's let a lot of people down here, Dana—

people who really love football, Dana,
who love to see bone-crunching hits, Dana,
and huge men knocking each other unconscious,
banging heads on the gridiron, Dana.

They just can't understand this kind of behavior.

Oh, Dana, Dana, Dana, Dana, Dana—

I mean, someone could have gotten seriously hurt.

I mean, here's Frickie, with his hand out like *this*—
like a special-needs kid at the petting zoo—
And I'm, like, *No, this is not happening.*
Frickie did not just step in it that deep.
But of course he did! Frickie *always* steps in it that deep!
LADIES AND GENTLEMEN, WE HAVE A RED LIGHT
AND WE SHOULD BE MOVING SHORTLY
And Frickie's like, "Whoa," like he's had a revelation,
and I actually started to think,
in spite of all the years that I've known Frickie,
in spite of the track record that goes by the name of Frickie,
that he's actually going to apologize—

And the night came down on us like a heavy wing.
And we walked through the shanty town of streets
tacked up at the feet of the towers of Manhattan.
The night came down on us and we walked fast,
the barely chained dogs of the traffic sniffing near us,
the barely chained dogs on each face passing
in the miles of night, and we tried to forget our boredom,
and we threw our ships on the first sea that washed up to us,
and we threw our words at whatever gods
were in the flight paths over us,
like Amelia Earhart calling her coordinates,
like children heaving rocks at the moon,
like grown men heaving rockets at the moon—

and he's like, "That is just *way* too much information."

How about *those* teeth, huh?

Well, for eating other dinosaurs, hon.

Because he was hungry, sweetie.

No, nothing eats people. That was just a movie.

No, that kind of thing doesn't happen, either, hon.

I don't care *what* your father said. *Or* Cynthia.
She's not your mother, you know that, right?

Well, things are very different in Afghanistan.

Well, for one thing, they're all religious wackos, honey.

Sweetie, this guy's been dead,
like, fifty million years, okay?
I don't really see what you're so afraid of here.

But in Hamdi, the Court said we could torch strange women.
The Court said we could nail up malcontents—
only, of course, if they aren't citizens.

The Court said we could fuck our kids—
not *literally* (except in certain cases).
The Court said we could survive on Coke and Twinkies.

In Hamdi, the Court said we could talk to God.
The Court said He's a decent Dude.
The Court said if we flapped our arms, we'd fly—

for the duration of the hostilities.

The Court said we could set enough nukes off
to split the earth, so the core oozed out and froze,
and still be well within our legal rights.

And the city is a crystal, is a toy—
near and distant, *clarified* by distance,

a battle cleansed by history and dark,
its plains and craters bright and sharp,

sharp as the moon that hovers, unimpeded,
trespassing on the black between penthouses—

Silent partner! unchanged by all this drama,
its silence unbroken by the rows of cabs passing,

unchanged from the time of the single cells, dividing,
tearing themselves in half to fit the future.

Your Reverence surely knows the score.
Your Reverence has read Machiavelli and Darwin.
Your Reverence has observed the praying mantis,
has witnessed the ocean receding under
the moon's inexorable draw, has seen
the virus under the microscope.
Your Reverence has seen what people do to each other
in off-shore prisons and trailer park bedrooms.

We are neither God nor Christ, Your Reverence.
We only insult them by such comparisons,
be it by word or deed.
We live as man in the world God made for us,
where survival of one means death of another,
where freedom of one means servitude of another,
where *the Lord doth put a difference
between the Egyptians and Israel*—[9]

where if one soul is to enter the blessed kingdom
another must writhe in the flames of hell
for all eternity, with no hope of reprieve.

Perhaps, Your Reverence, you and I
would not have chosen it this way. But choice,
as long as the Almighty reigns in heaven,
will never be man's lot. Your faithful servant

---

[9] *"But against any of the children of Israel shall not a dog move his tongue, against man
or beast: that ye may know how that the Lord doth put a difference between the Egyptians
and Israel."* Exodus, *11:7.*

unable to break free of the earth.

Did they just walk right over him?[10]
Do you think they saw him?
Did they run away when the police came?
Where's Haiti?
Where's Walmart?
What does Walmart look like?
Does anybody still go there?
What's a temp worker?

Tell me the story of the Romans.

How far is it from our house?
That's a long way, right?

Ms. Kasrel says, if you go far enough
you end up where you started.

But Calvin says you end up out in space.

---

[10] *Lines 1, 2, 3, 6, 10 and 11 are taken from an op-ed piece, "Bad Time Stories," Judith
Warner, 4 December 2008, The New York Times. The story is about a mother being
questioned by her seven-year-old daughter about Jdimytai Damour, trampled to death by
shoppers on November 28, 2008 at a Walmart in Valley Stream, New York.*

I guess it's time I actually said something, huh.
About all this. About all of you.
Old friends, new friends. The occasional asshole.
There's a theory going around that art is useless,
but I think I need only turn your attention
to this faucet sculpture to explode that myth.
Anybody thirsty? For a *faucet?*
Oh, man, I love you guys, I love this piece
with the afro made of pennies, to me it's worth—
It's genius, I mean, what else can you do
with that many pennies? It brings to mind a poem:

> The Emancipation Proclamation
> feels as good as masturbation.

Thank you. Thank you so much. I just wrote that one.
I'm very into rhyme, you know?
Actually, fuck rhyme. I just changed my mind.
I'm so glad you guys were here for this.
Call me Constantine, right? I mean, what was up
with *that* dude? Give me the God who helps me slaughter
the most people. Nice poster child
for Christianity, right? I'm sorry, folks,
what a boring topic. Where was I?
Battleground conversions. I think all poems
are battleground conversions. Right? I'm just kidding.
No, seriously, though. Take these lines by Oppen:

> Obsessed, bewildered

> By the shipwreck
> Of the singular

> We have chosen the meaning
> Of being numerous. [11]

---

[11] Of Being Numerous, *7, George Oppen.*

Actually, I have no idea what that poem means.
Bad example. But don't you just *feel*
that this guy is about to go careening down the hill
with his broadsword waving, shouting,
"We have chosen the meaning of being numerous!"
I don't have any idea what Oppen looked like,
but I tend to picture him as about six-eight,
two-sixty, ripped muscle, and black.
No, wait, that's Brandon Jacobs. His poetry
is running the fucking *football*, man. Just kidding.
That's ridiculous. I mean, a physical act
can't be a poem! Pretty soon
you'll be telling me this *shirt* is a poem—
and pretty soon—you're coming pretty close—
you'll be saying that mankind is completely irrelevant.

      Where were you when the towers fell?
      When Kennedy was shot?
      The first one?
      By that lone gun-mun?
      Wink, wink?
      No, seriously, though, where were you?

You see what I did there? Showed a poem
trying to exist in the real world, which
it can't, don't ask me why, the helmsman put it
down as law[12], and that's the source of its *tension*—
our dear friend, Alfred Lord Tension.
Because poetry makes nothing *happen* man.[13]
But can't you just *see* this guy, this guy
with bitten fingernails and wild eyes,
and a crown or whatever lords wear and you're, like,
arguing with your girlfriend and you look up
and Oh, man, there he is: Alfred Lord Tension!

---

[12] *"For the helmsman put it down as law / that we must suffer, suffer into truth."*
Agamemnon, *Aeschylus.*

[13] *"For poetry makes nothing happen,"* W.H. Auden, *"In Memory of W.B. Yeats."*

Bad in a life, awesome in a poem.
Words to live by, friends. Take global warming—
I'm starting to rant, aren't I.
I might as well be waving my broadsword around:
"We have chosen the meaning of being numerous!"
See how everything, in spite of your best efforts
to create chaos, just wants to gel together?
This is why you don't have to be smart to be a poet.
It's as easy as putting pennies on an afro, dude.
No offense—I love that sculpture. "Religion":

> The Buddha's bones are in the ground,
> but our Lord and Savior, Jesus Christ,
> His body can't be found.

Which nicely goes with *this* one, called,
"Poem Beginning with a Line by Oppen
and Ending with a Line by e.e. cummings":

> Obsessed, bewildered
> By the shipwreck of the singular,
> He spoke—and drank rapidly a glass of water.[14]

Oh, man. Oh, *man.* Now *that* is some good shit.
Though I just had the sudden urge to change that last line:
"He spoke—and drank rapidly a glass of *faucets.*"
No, sorry, that's awful. A glass of *faucets*? What the *fuck*?
I love the sculpture, though, man, I really do.
Don't ever change! Actually, I mean,
if you see a pattern in your work, smash it![15]
And if, oh if, there's a skeeter on your peter—[16]
Fuck! This guy needs *medication.*
He's, like, talking about himself in the third person.

---

[14] e. e. cummings, *"next to of course god america i."*

[15] *Pablo Picasso*

[16] *"If there's a skeeter on your peter, wack it off!" An old ditty.*

And now he's talking about himself talking
about himself in the third person. And *now*—
By the way, do you see what hell's like?
Do you still think it's so imperative
that you fornicate and touch yourselves
in unclean ways? Is damnation really worth
that moment of exquisite ecstasy,
so sublime you think you might be a god yourself,
trapped until now in the fetters of Manhattan—
That's the problem with conversions: you get *hooked*.
It's such a rush, changing what you believe—
if I could, I'd change what I believe
every second of the day—
We're all going to boil! No we're not! Yes we are!
I mean, right? I'm totally kidding. That would suck.

THE DEPTFORD TRILOGY by Robertson Davies

Lisa Abend

I recently re-read *The Deptford Trilogy*, by Robertson Davies. I am not normally a re-reader, but every now and then, I fasten on to a book. The first was Salinger's *Franny and Zooey*, which, for a brief period during my late teens and early twenties, I read annually. If, in hindsight, that seems an embarrassingly predictable choice for a suburban Jewish girl suffering from acute intellectual and spiritual pretension, I offer this defense: I wasn't reading for the story. When I choose to re-read fiction, it is not so much for the pleasure the novel brings (though it inevitably does) but for the wisdom it contains. I re-read books that I suspect have something to teach me about how to live.

I first read *The Deptford Trilogy* in graduate school, and despite the fact that (or perhaps because) it is an old-fashioned kind of novel, fell quickly in love with it. Although the three books that comprise the trilogy were published individually, they form a coherent whole not so much because they tell a single story, but rather because each of the stories departs from a single moment in time: when one boy in the grimly Calvinist, early twentieth century town of Deptford, Canada throws a snowball at another, and in missing, hastens the birth of a third. Each is narrated by a different man who took part in or was affected by that event, and if that seems thin soil in which to plant an entire trilogy, I can only say that you don't know Robertson Davies.

Davies is a graceful storyteller, writing with such a light hand—an elegant wit, and the unadorned language that one of his narrators (the one, in fact, who seems most closely to resemble Davies himself) calls plain speech—that you barely notice the metaphysical import behind the tale. Whether Dunstan Ramsay, a schoolteacher recounting how he came to be a respected hagiographer; David Staunton, an emotionally lost lawyer seeking Jungian analysis in order to understand his father and himself; or Magnus Eisengrim, a world famous magician recalling how he reinvented himself after an abusive childhood; Davies' narrators are all concerned with wonder and myth, the quest for the marvelous in a rational world. The appeal to a graduate student—especially one so previously enamored of Salinger—confronting stacks of critical theory should be clear.

This summer, I picked up the book again. And although I was immediately plunged back into the story with as much pleasure as before, I was startled to realize that the aspect that held me so captivated before—the emphasis on the mythical, on the world of wonders that lies behind the scrim of modern life (and that also happens to be the name of the cheap carnival where Eisengrim acquires his skill) no longer held my interest with the same intensity. Embarked on what can only be considered middle age, and having acquired a major career change and the usual bumps of adult life, I was drawn instead to the way, as Davies points out, each of his main characters shapes his own narrative. "We have all reinvented ourselves," Ramsay says at one point to the others, and you realize that all of us do the same thing. Meaning lies less in the events themselves than in how we string them together, and the well-lived life is one in which we examine our narratives, and accept them.

In what is perhaps my favorite passage, Ramsay again speaks:

> In the study of hagiography we have legends and all those splendid pictures of saints who killed dragons, and it doesn't take much penetration to know that the dragons represent not simply evil in the world, but their own personal evil as well.
>
> Of course, being saints, they are said to have killed their dragons, but we know that dragons are not killed; at best they are tamed and kept on the chain. In the pictures we see St. George, and my special favourite, St. Catherine, triumphing over the horrid beast, who lies with his tongue out, looking as if he thoroughly regretted his mistaken course in life. But I am strongly of the opinion that St. George and St. Catherine did not kill those dragons, for then they would have been wholly good and inhuman, and useless, and probably great sources of mischief, as one-sided people always are. No, they kept the dragons as pets.

It's a remarkable book, I think, that can speak with such power to the same person at two very different stages in her life. And I suspect that Davies' abilities extend even further. At one point in the first book, Ramsay meets up with a now elderly, but still wickedly intelligent Jesuit who, feeling somewhat alienated from the Jesus who died at age thirty-three, confesses to be searching "for a God who can teach me how to be old." Which means, I imagine, that I'll be picking up *The Deptford Trilogy* again. ❧

Open Late Hours

Zachary Watterson

One Sunday morning in 2009, I waited for an ex-con named Frank outside the International House of Pancakes. Twenty minutes late, Frank came walking around the corner in his faded red windbreaker pants, collared shirt, light jacket, sturdy boots, and a baseball hat over his silvery hair. The IHOP had been open all night. It was nearly empty when we stepped inside, out of the drizzle.

"Last night I had cinnamon rolls and pea soup."

"Nothing this morning?" Though I asked him the question, I nodded at a waitress coming around to the front from the kitchen.

"Nothing. But I've got enough only for coffee."

"I'll get your breakfast."

"You don't have to."

"Just don't worry about it."

Our waitress seated us at a corner booth and brought coffee. We ordered hash brown potatoes, scrambled eggs, and toast, all of which Frank could eat—soft foods. Frank had some of his lower teeth. His upper teeth were all gone. He was in his mid-fifties and looked ten years older. Creases like thumbprints marked pockets under his eyes. Crow's-feet branched toward his temples.

When my mother was pregnant with me, as part of her writing about the Pennsylvania state prison system, she brought me inside prisons and jails. One guy who was sort of a friend of my mother's had been convicted of murdering his wife and business partner. Frank was sort of a friend of mine. I'd met him when he was a prisoner at the county jail and I was his teacher. In addition to being a born-again Christian, Frank was also someone who knew about scrap metals: where to find them, how to sell them, and what the going rate was for various types.

"I used to have a lucrative scrap metal business."

"You had a shop?"

"Had a car and a truck. Went to this dumpster one time. The Lord directed me to go to this dumpster."

"How do you mean *directed* you?"

"This was in eighty-three." He poured sugar in his coffee and took a cautious sip. "Had just got done doing jail time for theft of stainless steel. I drove by rubbish piles, asphalt, dirt. They *did* have a no-trespass sign, but no one was there. I went every Saturday for seven Saturdays, took what I needed. During the week was working at a waterbed warehouse—minimum wage, and minimum wage wasn't paying the bills."

"I hear that," I said, "I've been working as an editor." That is, I was working as a managing editor for a scientific journal based at the university where I went to grad school, and I took a second job as staff at a halfway house for schizophrenics and other chemically imbalanced souls.

"Hard looking after money," Frank said. "I used to come home and give my wife most of it, let her pay the bills, ones we could afford."

"And she balanced the books, wrote the checks?"

"Nah. Cash only. I never trusted the banks."

"What were you saying about God directing you to that dumpster?"

"When I took that stuff from the dumpster, I said, 'Lord, if there's something wrong with me taking this stuff, let me know.' Well, I got a knock on my door, a Kent City cop."

"You got what you prayed for."

"I guess that's right. So I says to the cop, 'You wouldn't happen to be here about some scrap metal, would you?'" Frank sipped his coffee, and some kids, two teenagers with dyed neon hair, sat in a booth across the aisle. "The cop says yeah, that's what he's come for, and he's going to have to take me with him, and so we go for a drive." Frank frowned into his coffee, and I suspected he might have forgotten what he was saying, as sometimes happened, and say something about God's role in his scrapes with the law, but he surprised me and stayed with his story. "I told the judge I didn't mean to steal. I saw the no trespassing sign," Frank said, his voice rising. "But that stuff didn't belong to anybody—just dirt and rock."

"What did the judge say?"

"He was sympathetic. I told him I needed the money for my wife, the rent. When I got out of jail, I had half a tank of gas and no money. There was no food on the table, so I got down on my knees and prayed. I heard this voice: *Look in the dumpster across the street.* I was transported out of my body and was looking at the dumpster and I could see inside it where there was *a lot* of aluminum—at the time, aluminum was going for about twenty-two cents a pound—and there was some fiberglass and rods that had the EP Ski logo. I came back to my body, and got in my truck and drove over there."

"The aluminum was there?"

"It was enough to pay the rent, the light bill."

"Divine intervention," I said, probably sounding as dubious as I was.

"When I pray," Frank said, and pulled on his chin, "I see my spirit lifting up, and it's blue." He glanced out the window. "When I got saved it was like a ray gun out of Star Trek."

Here again was our waitress. She set our plates down, the eggs and hash brown potatoes steaming. I shook pepper on my eggs. Frank did the same, and added salt and ketchup. We ate, and through the rain-streaked windows to one side of our corner booth, I saw trucks swoosh by on

Madison. We ate without speaking, and there was the clatter of dishes from the kitchen and a low-pitched murmur of the voices of the other customers. The teenager with the nose ring bent over his plate, shoveling strips of syrupy pancakes into his mouth. Frank washed down his breakfast with more coffee. I settled the check, Frank added a dollar to the tip, and we pushed open the doors and walked out into the rain.

We walked east, then north. The rain fell from formidable clouds over the modest brick building, the First African Methodist Episcopal Church. Human forms—a man, whose angular face was the only part of him visible, and what looked like a woman from the shape of her blankets—lay on strips of cardboard, mostly sheltered from the rain, at the top of a short flight of stairs. The man sleeping there opened his eyes and I bid him good morning, and he gave me a nod, and having seen me, got somber again and closed his eyes. The sign on the church made clear my error: there was only one service on Sundays and we'd missed it. The church had the wrong information on its website. We agreed to meet the following Sunday, at the right time, for a service. Frank boarded a bus headed west for downtown. From there he caught a bus to West Seattle, where he stayed in an unheated room.

Next Sunday, the smell of rising dough wafted from the warm confines of a nearby bakery. The late summer air felt good on my neck. Churchgoers in fine clothes arrived in twos and threes. From a block away, I saw Frank in a shirt and trousers spotted with oil.

"I been working on tires," he said, "knocking out the rims." He had been stockpiling them to sell to a shop on Rainier Avenue.

We stepped inside First A.M.E. and followed a man in a blue suit up red-carpeted stairs. We took church bulletins—Xeroxed sheets—and entered the sanctuary. Not sure where to sit, I followed Frank. We took seats, on Frank's cue, seven rows from the pastors. We were the only whites in the pews. There were attractive black women in their twenties and thirties, elderly folks, and a handful of young women with their small children. I looked around at the small sea of faces. Some smiled, others cast suspicious glances, and still others appeared indifferent. Frank grabbed a Bible from a sleeve on the back of the pew.

Four pastors were seated in chairs that looked like thrones covered in what appeared to be satin. The chief pastor, a man of stentorian voice, delivered a sermon based on readings from the Gospel of John and the Acts of the Apostles; he spoke of "different tongues" and "eighteen languages." He held a red microphone, which matched the red décor of the church, near his lips. The church band began to play and the choir sang, clapped, and swayed. After the song, the pastor spoke.

"Any guests should please stand now and be acknowledged."

All eyes were on the two of us. Frank and I stood, the pastor said something, and though his words were garbled for me by the minor spectacle we had become and the ringing in my ears at having unexpectedly become the center of attention, the pastor's tone—warm and robust and welcoming—was clear to me and put me at ease. Once the pastor had thanked us and told us to be seated, the collection baskets were passed around and the choir sang again. One page of the program I was given at the door advertised the church's marriage ministry. Another page showcased a Pilates class promising "Fab Abs!" *Are You Ready to Melt the Muffin Top Before Thanksgiving? If you are, Fab Abs is here!!!*

On the program's last page was a word-find game.

The last time I saw a word-find game was when I was in the county jail, tutoring Frank. Prisoners who don't play these games can use them as currency in the jail's barter economy; I knew an inmate who traded another prisoner four word-find games for a cup of coffee from commissary.

We attended the fellowship hour in the church's basement. We ate cake, drank fruit punch, and Frank said something to the bass player from the church band.

"You play real well."

The man was big in the chest, a few inches taller than Frank. "Thanks."

"You ever heard of Robert Johnson?" Frank smiled at the man when he asked the question.

"Don't think so."

"He was a bluesman," I offered.

"That's right." Frank turned his attention to me. "I'm surprised *you* know that."

"You know what, Frank, you don't know much about me at all."

He waved his hand in the air between us. "Never mind."

"You don't ask questions."

"All right, kid. Never mind I said anything."

"Why were you *surprised?*"

"I was just surprised, that's all."

"Whatever." I laughed, and Frank laughed, and the bass player, who had been watching our little quarrel with amusement, joined in.

We chatted a little more with the bass player, ate cake, said so long, and went to the street. On our way to IHOP again, the wind was light and the sun was warm on our faces. In the light and the air, so welcome after a stretch in the clean, windless confines of the church, it occurred to me that Robert Johnson was the bluesman who sold his soul to the devil.

Less than a month later, Frank was back in jail and I sat waiting for him in a room that smelled like a jar of pennies. Greasy fingerprints, smeared across the partitions between prisoners in red uniforms and the rest of us, resembled viscous leakage discharged by snails. The room had three walls: each wall had five telephones on the visitors' side and five on the other side of the vitreous partitions; the partitions, naturally, separated non-prisoners from prisoners. On the free side, one woman cradled a phone to her ear; a second woman with dyed blond hair and a husky voice visited a man twice her size.

Frank, his hair grayish white, shorn close to his skull, his beard silvery, raised the phone on his side. "Listen." He cleared his throat. "So I was going to work for this lady, I had an hour and a half to get there."

"What are you telling me?"

"How I got arrested *this* time."

"All right."

"So I'm walking down the street."

"What street?"

"Do you want to know what happened?"

"Yeah."

"I'm walking down the street and I see two people arguing—behind a dumpster was spools of copper wire, fourteen gauge, small stuff, strand wire. Wasn't brand new. It had been open up and used . . . they were just scraps. Only had six bucks in my pocket—nearest metal company was six blocks away—noticed a garbage can, took the bag, loaded the spools, maybe forty or fifty pounds worth, started walking away."

"Who saw you?"

"Fire inspectors."

"And you . . ."

"I *ran.*"

"Carrying the garbage bag?"

"I dropped it. *Listen.* They called the police."

"Sure."

"Guy called me a piece of shit."

"One of the fire inspectors said that?"

"Yeah, and I thought about that. I shoulda told him, *I ain't a piece of shit. If I was, I'd be breaking into your house, fella.*"

We didn't say anything for a moment, and I could hear the women on either side of me talking to their men.

"I've been thinking of my brother," Frank said.

"Tommy?"

"Yeah." His brother Tommy died of AIDS in the early eighties. "Had a dream before Tommy died," Frank went on. "I was in an ocean of water. Like in Revelations, chapter thirteen, when the water is troubled and the beast comes out of the sea." Frank stared at the low part of the pellucid partition. "In my dream was a house. My dad had a hammer in his hand. He pulled one nail and the house burst open. Then I was in the water. I swam down and down. Down some more. And grabbed a worm with my mouth from the mud. There was water everywhere. I swam and swam until I was released into the Sound."

"You remember your dreams pretty well, then?"

"Yeah, I remember all that water."

And the beast? What I wanted to ask him as I sat there holding the telephone to my ear in the jailhouse waiting room was *Do you ever feel like that beast?* That question had been there for me—the fear that others would perceive me as less than human. It may have had something to do with growing up in the eighties in New York City, when people were getting shot to death on my street. In my memory there were more murders in the wintertime, and I remember hearing gunshots at night and in the morning seeing blood in the snow. My father told me stories of our family that made me aware of the monstrous capabilities of human beings: In the 1880s, high in the Carpathian Mountains in the village of Koselova, Hungary, in a house between a synagogue and a river, my great-great grandmother, Esther Itzkowitz, had a brother named Heshel.

In the winter of 1882, Heshel fell in the river. A doctor sawed his frostbitten legs below his knees. In 1900, Esther sailed to America and worked as a cook on Manhattan's Lower East Side. As an émigré, Esther lived another decade after learning Nazis had marched into Koselova and murdered her brother Heshel and the whole of Koselova's Jewish citizenry. Here in the jailhouse in 2009, on my side of the partition, I was beginning to see what I had not seen before: my detachment from Frank and my caretaking of him. I saw that what Frank and I had was not at all a reciprocal friendship. I was very different in temperament and personality from Frank, I thought, and at that moment I realized he was talking to me.

"Losing my wife changed me," Frank went on. He had been talking, saying something I didn't hear, while I was ruminating, and now he was going on with a story the first part of which I'd missed. But he didn't seem to notice my lapse. I listened to what he was saying now: "I didn't know where I was. I got out of jail and told God, *I've been doing it Your way. Now I'm going to party.*"

"How long did the party last?"

"Too long." Frank's eyes were bloodshot, explosive yet weary. "We buried my grandmother. We waked her in her house. Until then, I'd never touched heroin. My aunt Betty was into it. Betty was married to a guy named Mitch who robbed drug stores. Then Mitch got clean and began leading a Narcotics Anonymous meeting in the North End."

"Quite a change."

Frank squinted at the shelf at his elbow. He was a prisoner trying to make sense of his life, and I was on the free side of the walls, trying to understand why I was still free. I wondered what it meant that I had committed crimes—petty theft, drugs, trespassing, vandalism—and had never been caught, while guys like Frank had spent much of their lives in a cage.

"About my wife . . . ."

"What about her?"

"Besides her I had a lot of tough ones."

"Tough relationships?"

"Yeah, a while ago I was hanging on to a drug-related relationship. We bought crack in the jungle. Slept in the green belt. Saw an owl. It had a giant head on him. He was perched there looking down on us. We were caught up in the addiction, me and Susan. Sometimes I still have the urge to splurge."

"On what?"

"Heroin. I've smoked crack. Don't understand how people enjoy it. How can you enjoy seeing spiders and rats? I get the paranoia. I put a towel under the door so the cameras can't snake under it. Then I start thinking the cameras are coming through the keyholes." Frank laughed once, hard. His pale-blue eyes were grayer than I'd seen them. He closed his eyes, pointed his index finger and middle finger, and pressed his fingertips against his eyelids.

"Been getting migraines—shooting pains in my head."

"Hmm."

"It's the lights."

"I could see how that could get to you."

"And the stale air."

"Dries out your skin."

"My feet and hands, too."

"Um, you, uh, get enough water?"

"It tastes like swimming pool water, chlorinated."

"Yuck."

"This morning some televangelist was talking about the Book of Daniel. It's right before the Book of Hosea, Old Testament. Well, this guy in the tank says, 'You said it was New Testament.' 'No,' I say, 'I said it was Old.' And I start laughing 'cause the whole thing is kind of comical."

"How was it comical?"

"We were playing pinochle and the guy wanted a fight."

Card games were a welcome distraction for Frank; he played pinochle and spades. Each *tank*—a unit of space that contained inmates—held twenty-four prisoners on cots fixed immovably to the floor, as well as a toilet, a telephone, a television, and a card table.

"And that was funny."

"I'm not a great martial artist." Frank rolled his shoulders, imitating a fighter, and raised the hand not holding the phone. "I got my old techniques, I don't want to hurt nobody anyways. I was having a hard time shuffling the deck. The cards were old. I can't see too well without my glasses. The guy got offended, wanted to make an issue out of nothing. I told him, 'You got to take a look at yourself and take some inventory— now here you're trying to act like Billy Badass in front of everyone in the tank.' The guy's a clown. Not someone searching for God in an honorable way, searching for what the Lord wants him to do in this life." A guard's voice came over the phone, an announcement that visiting hours had ended, and the line went dead.

When Frank got out of jail, I didn't hear from him. Months later, when I next found him, Frank was on the seventh floor. The seventh floor of the King County Jail was where the "ding biscuits," jail vernacular for the "mentally ill," were housed. He had shrunk. The jail-issue uniform hung off his skeletal arms, and we spoke over phones mounted in the wall between us. He squatted, hopped to a half-stand, rubbed a hand over his unkempt beard, looked away. He couldn't seem to focus. Had a lack of heroin and an abundance of stale air enervated him? Whatever the reason, he was jittery.

"They said my heart rate was too low," he said. "Said I might die. They had the hospital come over to pick me up." His face was wan. His skin had an anemic, sickly pallor. "One of the problems," he said, "is going to sleep on the bus. I go past where I'm headed. The woman I was staying with in West Seattle does a good job of sounding so sweet but she's very manipulative. It's like I'm in that movie with James Caan. *Misery*."

"Hmm."

"I'm walking on thin ice around here."

"Sorry to hear that."

"I'm scared. It's a touchy situation, my mind is mixed up."

"Like how?"

"It's like somebody is trying to manipulate my life."

"I see." His paranoia didn't surprise me, since I had seen flashes of his craziness before. But now it somehow struck me with greater force that, against my own wishes, I was becoming increasingly leery of him.

"How are your headaches?"

"Don't get 'em now."

"That's a good thing."

"I been on the methadone. I'm tired. My eyes are burned out. Was working in the kitchen on the fourth floor."

"You been eating?"

"Not much. The devil is having a time of messing up my life."

"Ah."

"See this," he said, lifted one leg, raised his pants, and revealed the rib of a thick scab on his ankle where the skin was recently torn.

"*Oww*. How did that happen?"

"The GPS thing I had to wear around my ankle—it cut into my leg, got infected. They put me on an antibiotic."

"I hope—" I said, but the line had gone dead.

No "so long," no "see you some other time." Outside the jail, I walked past sculptures at the front of the building, and was reminded of children's toys: blocks, triangles, chairs, glitter; purple and green tiles lined the plaza, ribbons of aqua and violet. It was after ten at night, dark, a cold wind rising off the Sound. The jail's windows were not really windows, I noticed, but horizontal breaks, darkened mesh-covered wire, inconspicuous fenestration. I turned the corner east on James Street and the clamor of Interstate 5 thundered above. South on Sixth Avenue, a camera—mounted over a vast sliding gate that opened for police cruisers, vans and vehicles—swiveled. The gate admitted a cruiser, then closed, and on Jefferson I walked west down the hill toward the water.

It was fall, nearly winter, when I next took a seat in the west visiting room. Frank came in and sat across from me. He looked better—less anxious, heavier.

"They gave me fifty days, there's time served, so I get out next Tuesday."

"Nice."

"Yeah, I want to start my business over again. But I worked two full days and my boss didn't pay. Not the full amount."

"What will you do when you get out?"

"I want to get my driver's license." Frank fiddled with a Band-Aid covering a weal the size of a quarter on his forearm, maybe a burn. "I'm going to need a receipt book for what I buy and one for what I sell. I'm thinking of having a business that's open when banks aren't. It's going to be mostly cash. Open late hours." He quit worrying his burn with the hand not holding the phone. "I'd have early morning hours, then a long break before evening hours. I'll do business from a warehouse where I can bring the vehicles I buy at the auction on Aurora. I'll get into motor homes and start building trailer homes. Then I'll buy some land—a corner lot. It's got to be big enough. The cash flow is going to be one of those tough issues. Before, when I had my business, I had customers I could count on. When I was at the end of my marriage I had two guys working for me. Then, after things fell apart, I started making real money. If it wasn't for my wife, I could've been a millionaire by now." He must have seen my smirk, since he added, "I'm serious."

"A millionaire?" I hadn't meant to smirk, but then it was hard to imagine Frank as a millionaire. For instance, where would he keep the money? He was suspicious of banks. Would he store it under the bed? But who was I to laugh? I wore a sweater-vest knitted for me by my wife and the Johnston & Murphy shoes I wore on the day we were married. Straighten up, I told myself, think about what it might be like to walk a mile in Frank's boots.

Frank went on about how he could've been a millionaire.

"Once I've got my land," he said, "I can have my employees living on it."

"All right."

"But about my wife, she wouldn't let me do what I wanted."

Frank talked as if he was glad to be rid of his ex-wife, but the truth lurking behind the façade was clear: he was a prisoner, the winter was wet and cold, the thin jail uniform would not keep him warm. He would have limited coffee and food and fresh air. His time was running out.

But Frank *needed*, for the solace of the illusion, to convince himself that his future would be paved with gold. "I've been wanting to work on magnetic propulsion," he said, and pounded the shelf on his side of the partition with his fist. "I've got a motor that works on magnets. Money is an issue."

"Always is."

"Time is another issue."

"Yeah, well—"

"I'm looking at the money and time involved, and it's clear I need to build a generator. All I have to do is get an alternator and the belt of a ten-speed bicycle. Then I need a serpentine belt and I'd hook it up to the alternator. I'd drill magnets into the wheel. The two north polarities would push against each other and the south polarities would push against each other. Then I'd need some brake calipers, and I'd drill magnets into the brake itself. That's a million-dollar invention. It could be a multi-million-dollar invention."

As I walked away from the jail and through the rain, Frank's hyperbole sank into my imagination until I could picture him living in a palace on a hill, surrounded by mermaids and towers and spires. In this phantasmagoria of Frank's kingly paradise, he sold his invention to a major American auto-manufacturer, who in turn sold him a pickup truck. Frank drove his truck to scrap yards, loaded aluminum and copper and iron, and with these metals and alloys he fashioned a kingdom on the foundation of the world. (Written in the Book of Matthew, Frank once told me, were these words: *Then shall the King say unto them on his right hand, Come, ye blessed of my Father, inherit the kingdom prepared for you from the foundation of the world.*) In Frank's empire, all outlaws and madmen and thieves shared the food and drink of their king, future generations sang of Frank's canny and courage in the face of poverty and powerlessness, and songs and odes and threnodies were written to praise and mourn and celebrate the magnanimity and nerve of the outlaw-king who salvaged scrap from dumpsters and coaxed into form a kingdom by the sea. At an intersection, I stood and watched traffic zip past me and disappear in a winding tunnel that connected to I-5. The crossing signal told me I could walk, so I took a step, began walking toward the far curb, and though I did not—and do not—believe in God, I said a prayer for Frank. Did Frank say a prayer for me? I didn't think so. I walked away from the jail that evening, wanting not to see him again. I thought how wrong Rousseau was. Humans are not inherently good. We are capable of some good and some evil and many shades and hues that are neither good nor evil but something else entirely. ❧

Big Ray, or Some Things Concerning My Childhood, with an Emphasis on My Father

Michael Kimball

My parents didn't have very much money the first few years after they moved back to Michigan. I was too young to remember that time, of course, but apparently we lived in a series of rental houses that were identified by their particular infestations. We lived in the mice house, the spider house, the raccoon house, and the cockroach house. My father remembers turning the lights on before entering any room. My mother remembers leaning over my crib and wiping bugs off my forehead.

Once, my parents couldn't get me to stop crying. They couldn't figure out what was wrong with me. My mother says my father talked her into ignoring me. He said I would stop crying if they stopped picking me up and trying to comfort me.

After a few days, my mother took me to the doctor, who thought I might have an ear infection. I didn't, but I did have a spider living inside my right ear.

There's a photograph of my father and me lying in my parents' bed. I'm about two years old and I'm lying where my mother usually was in their bed. The sheet is pulled up over our stomachs and our hands are on top of it. My father and I are turned toward each other and smiling at each other. I'm trying to remember what that must have felt like.

Not long after that photograph was taken, my sister was born. My father didn't make it to the hospital for her birth, either. He was deer hunting with his younger brother somewhere in the woods of Northern Michigan. The same day my father brought home the carcass of a six-point buck, my mother brought home my week-old sister.

I don't know who took care of me during that time when I was two years old and neither one of my parents were at home. I don't think I was left at home on my own.

Not long after that, there's a photograph of my father sitting on the couch. He's holding my sister in his arms and has his face turned down toward hers. I'm sitting at the other end of the couch in nearly the same posture—my arms folded across my chest, my face turned away, looking at something outside the frame. I wasn't old enough to understand what was happening in the family, but I already seemed to know that my sister was the favorite.

There's a photograph of me opening presents on Christmas morning, 1970. I'm smiling and holding up a new pair of black cowboy boots. I'm so happy that I'm holding the cowboy boots out to the camera. My father is behind me in the photograph, sitting off to the right. He is staring back at me with a blank look on his face. He is either really tired or he doesn't care.

I wonder if my father didn't like it when I was happy.

There's a photo of me from when I'm about four years old. My mouth is dropped open and I'm looking at my father with a facial expression that's some mixture of surprise, hurt, bafflement, and disappointment. It may have been my father's version of teasing me—which could be brutal or devastating, but never fun or funny—but I don't know what exactly my father had just done to me that particular time or why my mother felt the need to capture it with a photograph.

My father is still thin in all those photographs, but I don't ever remember him looking like that. When I see him thin, I think it's a different person. I feel like I had a different father than the one in those photographs.

I went through a stage where I would walk into whatever room my father was in and turn the lights off. I never told anybody why, but I was trying to make him disappear.

My father would call out when he came home from work, and, when I was a little boy, this was an exciting time in the house. For a time, my sister and I would run to the front door and hug his leg or jump up and down around him. My father standing just inside the front door having just come home from work, that was one of my happiest memories for a time.

It was around this time I noticed my mother wasn't as happy about my father's daily homecoming as my sister and I were. Often, she wouldn't hug him or go to the front door or even say anything to him. If my mother didn't greet my father in any way, which happened enough for me to notice it, then he would wait until my sister and I let go of him and say something mean to my mother. Then it would get really quiet. I remember looking back and forth between my mother and my father until it felt scary.

Here's one of the insults I remember: *Your mother seems to be lost in thought. It's someplace she's never been before.* My father would laugh and get my sister and me to laugh with him. It was confusing that things could be funny and mean at the same time.

My mother and my father were really good at being mean to each other. Sometimes, when my father stood up, my mother would look at him and say, *I always wanted a taller husband.*

The thing I remember most about the taller insult was how it filled me with a strange feeling of power. I was just a little boy and I was going to grow bigger and get taller. I made a pact with myself to grow up to be taller than my father. It felt like something I could control.

My father used to find different ways to insult my mother. He would say things like, *You wouldn't be so ugly if you were a redhead.* Or, *Are you always this stupid or is today a special occasion?*

At the time, I didn't understand these insults. I could see how much he liked her when he looked at her.

Sometimes, when my father came home, my mother would say, *I was hoping you were somebody else.* She would usually say it with a really pretty voice, which made it confusing, but pretty soon my mother and my father would start arguing, and that would turn into the kind of yelling that was too loud and too fast to follow.

Sometimes, I think that was how I learned to talk—loud and fast. I don't know why none of the other adults I was around ever corrected me. It was my kindergarten teacher, Mrs. Fisher, who taught me how to use my quiet voice.

In my family, it was usually the last person talking who won the argument, but my father could also win any argument by raising his hand back over his head. The only consolation was that his hand was usually open-palmed and not a fist.

I tried it on my mother once, but it didn't work. She sent me to my room.

Once, my parents had an argument because my mother set out slices of bread with dinner instead of dinner rolls. My father knocked over his chair when he stood up from the dinner table. He made the whole house shake when he slammed the back door on his way out of the house.

For my father, good bread was an important distinction between the poor farm family he grew up in and the middle class family he expected us to be. That is why we had family dinners on Sundays. That is why we ate so many pot roasts.

My father could fight about anything—bread, haircuts, light bulbs, newspapers, cats, boots, chicken, belts, pickles, chairs, lottery tickets, playing cards, potato chips, cheese and crackers, socks, aftershave, dishes, combs, loose change—anything.

When I was a boy, long before I had four knee surgeries, I used to love to run. Every weekday evening around 5:30, I waited at the end of the block for my father's pickup truck to turn the corner onto our street and then raced him to the driveway of our home. I used to think, *Can't he see how fast I am?*

I used to be a boy with a father.

During the mid-1970's, there was a gas crisis. People stopped buying as many cars and trucks, and companies like Diamond Reo had to lay off workers, including my father. A lot of fathers in our neighborhood lost their jobs then, and the summer of 1975 was strange with so many of them at home so much of the time. Most of us had never had our fathers pay so much attention to us and we didn't quite know what to do. We still played baseball and basketball and rode our bikes up and down the street, but one father would come out to throw us some pitches or shoot jumpers, and then another father would, and pretty soon it would turn into these brutal father-son contests that didn't end until somebody got hurt.

In the fall of 1975, my father started working as a safety inspector for a company called the Accident Fund. There was all kinds of gear that came with his new job—plastic helmets with face shields, eye goggles with a thick rubber strap, long rubber gloves, and different colored ear plugs. I had no idea what my father did with those things when he went to that job. I didn't understand how somebody could inspect safety. It seemed more likely that my father somehow caused accidents, but I didn't understand how that could be a job somebody would get paid for. Sometimes, when my father left the gear around the house, I would run around with it on. It made me feel like a person from the future.

Years later, I learned my father's job was to make companies install safety protocols to keep people from getting hurt at work. I don't want to talk about how ironic that is, but what if he would have done that at home too?

I remember the few times my father and I played catch. I can still see the baseball in the air between us.

Also, I always liked it when he came home from work and I was playing basketball in the driveway. I would pass my father the basketball and he would throw up a two-handed set shot before going into the house. He almost always missed and I would chase after the ball.

One Saturday afternoon, my father took me to a shooting range. After a gun safety class, I got to shoot his rifle, a 30-30 Winchester. I remember two things about that time: (1) I missed the target by so much we had no idea where the bullet went. (2) The kickback from the rifle made my shoulder hurt for days. I still don't know what my father was trying to teach me that afternoon.

One of the other things I remember doing with my father was playing cards—Gin rummy, cribbage, Euchre, War—any game that could be won or lost. He taught me to play cards, in part, because my mother didn't like cards and wouldn't play with him. I was just the next available body, but it still made me feel special. It felt like he had chosen me.

I was ten years old when my father taught me how to play poker. That first time, he told me to go get my piggy bank and he'd teach me a new game. We emptied my piggy bank and split up my life savings. I didn't understand why we were only playing with my money—especially since I knew there was a pile of change on top of his dresser—but I still wanted to play. The game was five card draw and I understood which hands were better than other hands, but I didn't understand when to bet, raise, or fold at the right times. That afternoon, I lost all my money to my father and developed a great need to beat him. I learned how much I liked gambling and how much I didn't like my father.

I wanted to play poker again, but my father didn't give me any of my money back. He left all my change on his side of the kitchen table and I knew I couldn't take any of it back even though he had used half of my life savings to win the other half of my life savings from me. I put my empty piggy bank back in my bedroom and thought about how I would play my hands the next time.

Over time, my father taught me how to play five card draw, five card stud, seven card stud, Texas hold'em, Omaha, Omaha high-low, lowball, and other variations on poker. We never used wild cards. My father didn't like the way they changed the odds.

Once, for his birthday, I bought my father scratch off lottery tickets. After he scratched all of them off—and didn't win anything—he told me I bought the wrong ones.

One of the grossest memories I have of my father is him making breakfast. He would stand over a frying pan wearing nothing but tight, stretchy, red bikini briefs. His underwear was always too small for him, so the crack of his butt stuck out above the waistband and his stomach fat hung down over the front. The grease would spit and pop in the frying pan. He would stick one hand in his underwear and scratch himself in a way that couldn't be ignored while he worked the spatula with his other hand. He liked his eggs greasy and over easy. He fried his bacon until it was burnt.

When I was a little boy, my disgust mechanism would kick in and I wouldn't be able to finish my breakfast. I would get in trouble for that, but I would get up and leave the kitchen anyway. Even today, the smell of greasy eggs still makes me feel queasy.

After my father died, I was remembering the underwear and the eggs with my sister and she was dumbfounded. The smell of greasy eggs makes her sick too. Her therapist wonders if that smell is a trigger for something that happened to us, but neither one of us can remember what happened after we left the kitchen.

My father's life was an ordinary one in so many ways. I wonder if I am making him into something more than he was because he was my father.

At the back of my father's sock drawer, under some dress socks he never seemed to wear, there was a black-and-white photograph with scalloped edges that had curled up over the years. The photograph was a close-up, two sets of fingers pulling apart something hairy and fleshy and slick. I found the photograph when I was six years old. I didn't realize what it was until years after that.

There is about a seven-year gap when there aren't any photographs of my father. During this time, he grows sideburns and gets fat. The next time we see my father, he is standing on the patio behind our house wearing a black tank top and grilling hamburgers. His face is glistening with sweat in nearly the same way the hamburgers are glistening with fat on the grill. This is the father I remember: Big Ray.

My father loved to barbecue and it didn't even have to be summer for him to go out on the patio and light up the grill. He would even stand out there during the winter—in his shirtsleeves, no coat—turning over the hamburger patties and strip steaks with a pair of tongs until the meat was burnt on both sides. He didn't like even a hint of blood in his cooked meat. The fire colored his face mean.

Sometimes, in the mornings before school, my father would look at the way I was dressed and say, *Looking sharp.* That always made me feel really good.

There's a photograph of my father sitting at a picnic table and holding up an empty plate. He looks pretty happy in that shot.

Once, my mother and sister and I were all sitting at a picnic table—with the summer food all lined up in the middle—and we were waiting for my father before we started eating. He sat down on one end and the whole picnic table tipped—the food all sliding toward him and onto the ground before he could stand back up. What I'm trying to say is this: all three of us together wasn't enough against my father.

My father broke furniture. There were certain chairs my father did not sit on. Every couch that was ever in our house eventually had a small stack of bricks under the frame where it had cracked so people could still sit on it without sliding into the middle. My parents' bed had two-by-fours laid across the bed frame to support the cracked box springs and keep the mattress from sagging into the middle too.

Sometimes, I feel like my father is sitting in the chair next to my desk. He's a ghost now and thinner. I'm not worried about him breaking the chair.

My mother took my sister and me to church every Sunday morning, but my father never went with us. He always stayed home in bed with the newspaper and I couldn't figure out why my father wasn't worried about going to hell. How could he not be afraid of Our Heavenly Father? Eventually, I asked him if he believed in God and his answer was halting and awkward. His botched response was the first thing to make me wonder if God actually existed and I realized I might not have to be afraid of God either.

It took me longer to realize I didn't have to be afraid of my father.

My father used to do this thing when we were in public and he didn't want to be seen yelling at me or hitting me. He would put his arm around me and rest his hand on my shoulder in a way that must have looked affectionate to anybody who saw it. Then he would grip some muscle in my shoulder so hard that it would make me seize up. The gesture must have made him look like a good father, but I wouldn't be able to move or talk or even scream out in pain.

I will still startle if somebody puts an arm around my shoulder that way.

Once, after my father had knocked me down over something, I got back up, ran at him, and launched my whole body toward his midsection. I was trying to ram him or tackle him, something like that, do as much damage as I could. I felt like this action was somehow going to change things between us, but I just bounced off my father and fell back down, my arms open and empty. He didn't move, except to lift one of his feet and kind of nudge my shoulder with it.

Another time, I left a drinking glass on an end table and my father told me to pick it up and take it into the kitchen. For some reason I don't remember and can't explain, I refused to do it. My father hit me and told me again to pick it up. I refused again and he hit me again. I remember standing there, not moving and not saying anything as he hit me over and over again. Right then, I didn't feel like there was anything my father could do to really hurt me. I felt like I could absorb so much pain and still walk away from it.

One of the things I found in my father's papers was the program from his 25th high school reunion. There is a little biography for everybody in the class of 1957 and my father's says he worked *in engineering* at Diamond Reo—even though he worked as a draftsman. It also says he was working as a safety *engineer*—even though he was a safety *inspector*. My father wasn't what he wanted to be. My father wasn't what I wanted him to be either.

After my first girlfriend broke up with me, my father told me I would have lots of girlfriends even though I was pretty sure then I would never have another girlfriend. After he said that, he handed me an old copy of *Playboy* magazine from his stack on the top shelf of the closet. He said, *Pictures of naked girls aren't as much trouble as real girls.*

That was supposed to be some kind of advice and it was one of two times my father gave me any kind of advice. The other time was after I came home from a date with a girl named Ellen Bonner. He was drunk and said, *I recommend the blowjob. Nobody ever got pregnant from a blowjob.*

My father hated it when I talked on the telephone to Ellen Bonner, especially when it was a school night. We only had one telephone and if anybody talked on it for more than a couple of minutes, my father would start screaming about the line needing to be open. He thought somebody else might be trying to call the house even though nearly everybody knew they weren't supposed to call our house after dark. For a while, I did as he said, but, eventually, I wanted to talk to Ellen Bonner more than I feared what my father might do to me if I didn't get off the telephone.

Sometimes, my mother would stand in the kitchen next to the telephone and kind of guard it from my father, but there wasn't much she could do to save me from him. I had never really defied my father before, but I would turn away from him as he screamed at me. I would hold the telephone tight to one ear and the palm of my hand over my other ear. I could still hear my father yelling at me and Ellen Bonner could hear him yelling through the telephone, but we would keep talking like it wasn't happening.

At some point, I started stretching the telephone cord across the kitchen and talking to Ellen Bonner outside on the patio. It helped having the sliding glass doors between my father and me. I could still see him and hear him, but the glass between us made it seem as if it wasn't real— as if it was something I was watching happen on the television or a movie screen.

I knew I was usually going to get a beating when I came back inside the kitchen and hung up the telephone, but that only happened when my father was still awake. Sometimes, I would stay on the line with Ellen Bonner as long as I could just to postpone the beating. Sometimes, she would have to hang up, but I would keep talking and listening as if she was still on the other end of the line. Other times, my father would fall asleep on the couch in the living room and I could sneak up to my bedroom without getting any kind of beat down.

I don't know why my father waited for me to hang up the telephone instead of just holding down the cradle so we were disconnected. All I can think of is that my defiance gave him an excuse to beat me, which he seemed to want to do and which somehow seemed acceptable to me at the time.

Eventually, I started to fight back even though I wasn't big enough or strong enough to do any real physical damage to my father. I was still just a skinny teenage boy and my father was a full-grown man. Plus, my father weighed double what I did then, and he also had really fast hands. It usually didn't last too long and he usually didn't leave marks on me. There were almost never any cuts or bruises on my face or on the lower parts of my arms, nothing that could be seen above my collar or below my short sleeves.

Sometimes, I landed a punch on his arms or in his stomach, but I'm not sure he ever felt those. One time, I knocked the wind out of him when I kicked him in the chest as I was running up the stairs trying to get away from him. Another time, I caught him with an elbow in the neck. It was really satisfying to hear him gasp for breath and see him hold his neck with both of his hands as if he was choking himself.

The beatings didn't stop until after the time my father fell backwards down the stairs and hit the back of his head on the landing. He looked crumpled at the bottom of the stairs and he always stood with a little hunch after that. I felt a little stronger and a little taller than I had just before that happened.

Sometimes, I still get the urge to fight my father. If my father weren't dead, I would kick his ass.

My relationship with my father shifted after the beatings stopped. I was eighteen years old and I started calling him *Big Ray*. For some reason I can't explain, my father seemed to think me calling him the nickname made him cool.

Another thing: I stopped bringing any of my girlfriends around the house because of the way my father looked at each of them—always staring at different body parts, but not really looking at their faces. I watched him stare at Melanie Durbin as she sat down and then as she stood up— always trying to get a glimpse up a skirt or down a top. He saw me catch him, but he didn't stop, and I became afraid for her, too.

When I was a teenager, I learned how to leave a room whenever my father entered it. The timing of this was important. It had to be done while he was still sitting down or getting settled. We got along much better that way.

In 1985, my parents celebrated their 25th wedding anniversary. My mother's maid of honor threw a big party and I didn't understand how everybody was so happy for them. In front of everybody, my father gave my mother a huge emerald ring, which seemed to confuse her. She seemed to be wondering if he might actually love her in a way she had forgotten. But the emerald ring was just an extravagant gesture, a kind of performance my father was so good at outside the house, the loving husband and the good father.

After I graduated from high school, I moved out of the house and hours away for college. I only saw my father on certain holidays, a couple of winter breaks and spring breaks, and one summer when I couldn't find a job at college. I don't know as much about my father after I got away. I felt terrible about leaving my sister behind.

Sometimes, I try to figure out how different I might have been if my father had been nicer to me. Would I try as hard as I do? Would I be happier than I am? Would I have a different wife? Would I have children instead of cats? Would I be a schoolteacher instead of a writer? Would I ever have moved away from home? Would I be more sad, but less torn up?

After college, I moved even farther away from home and stopped going home for holidays. I stopped calling home too. I became so busy with my own life that I began to forget my father. ↝

Recommending KING DRIFTWOOD

Rimas Uzgiris

I first encountered Welshman Robert Minhinnick at a poetry reading in Upper Manhattan. He wouldn't speak to the audience before beginning, not even when he couldn't find his briefcase—he had the event organizer ask the audience if they had seen it. Then, manuscript found, he began, his voice instantly intense, committed, mesmerizing. He spoke with a Welsh accent, and each word came out molded precisely for the emotion of the line, sometimes soft, sometimes rising, intense. That voice echoed in my mind long after the event, and I continue to hear it as I re-read *King Driftwood* (Carcanet Press, 2008).

Oracular, expansive, and inclusive, the poetry of Robert Minhinnick reminds me of Walt Whitman, transplanted to coastal Wales, yet open to the entire world. Little known on this side of the pond, "The Castaway" was short listed for the Forward Prize for best poem in the UK in 2004; in 2003, "The Fox in the National Museum of Wales," another poem from this collection, won the same award. It impresses itself on the mind with memorable alliteration:

> The fox is in the fossils and folios, I cry.
> The fox is in the Photography and the Folk Studies Department.
> The fox is in the flux of the foyer,
> The fox is in the flock.

His poems teem with natural details: goldfinches, crabs, dolphins, scurvygrass, samphire. One also encounters the human element: small-town eccentrics, mushroom gatherers, solitary wanderers. But, impressively, his poems stretch far beyond the Welsh coastline to include Iraq and Lithuania, Charles Saatchi and Glenn Gould, iPods and atomic energy. Despite this, reading his work, I never feel scattered or lost because everything matters, down to the last detail of a bombing in Iraq or seagrass on the coast.

"The Cormorant" is characteristic of what I consider Minhinnick's best work, with its love of nature, criticism of an overreaching, warlike humanity, stunning metaphoric leaps (the bird becomes both soul and cruise missile), and a tone both personal and oratorical. In the poem, the bird carries with it the mark of humanity's hubris:

> But here you come again,
> stealth-bomber out of the empty

quarter, trailing your own death
across the sky, in your heart
the ashes of American astronauts,
your forgiveness one black feather
taking a lifetime to drift
down from the stratosphere.

Minhinnick's poetry is not a solipsistic dwelling in consciousness, nor concerned with language for its own sake, nor with the poet's successes and failures in life. Instead, he incessantly pours himself outwards towards the external world. Often this leads to a critical stance. In "An Isotope, Dreaming" he reflects, bitterly, on the Iraq war:

And no, I don't feel sorry for your boys.
Let them anoint their blisters
with Exxon's frankincense,
wipe their arses with figs,
tip the bottles of bullets to their lips
and taste the pomegranate beer of old Shiraz.
We all sign up for something.

Stylistically, Minhinnick's techniques are diverse, albeit unified by voice and vision. In a single, long poem one can encounter stanzas that rhyme, lines that repeat, prose-like sections, and lines that break apart under the strain of their content:

The g
    the gg
        the ga
        the gamma
    the game
the gamma
    ghosting towards
        the cell's gateway.

This is poetry of myriad expressive devices, engaged with the world in all its diversity, convinced it has something important to say—to safeguard, to save.

    ॐ

Prologue, a Letter: the Twin & Her Lover, Lacan & the Other

Addie Tsai

a. I wrote a poem about a lover that contained the lines: *When does the language/of the body—that roundness/of physical response—//drop the dead?* and *Our bodies, silent, lift triangles/of light, dying, dying.*

b. This lover was the only poet I ever dated the old-fashioned way, and the first man to suspect that I was, in fact, making love to the wrong gender: *It is clear you are not at all interested in the penis.*

c. *Le petit mort*, or *little death*, is a metaphor for *orgasm*.

d. According to Wikipedia, *it can refer to the spiritual release that comes with orgasm, or a short period of melancholy or transcendence, as a result of expenditure of the* life force.

e. Again according to Wikipedia, *the term can also be used when some undesired thing has happened to a person and has affected them so much that* a part of them dies inside.

f. When I wrote those lines, I was thinking of how hard it is, when fucking, to erase those other dead lovers that came before. But now that I read it again, I marvel at the loss I felt giving my body to men, how each occurrence was a slow and painful taking away. *Desire is neither the appetite for satisfaction nor the demand for love, but the difference that results from the subtraction of the first from the second, the phenomenon of their splitting.*—Lacan

g. When I wrote this poem, I had never before heard of *le petit mort.*

h. When Gene first put his mouth to my sister's still forming lips, what died?

i. It is true that I have loved my sister, and it is true that I have betrayed her.

j. Emma is convinced of one, but not the other.

k. Lacan says that *man's desire is the desire of the Other.*

l. *Which basically means that we are always asking the Other what he desires.*

m. I have been thinking of all the little deaths in this scenario, how the love between us, as twins and as lovers, sank into the moist earth, earth that was moist with her body, black at first, then gradually growing colorless and stale.

n. I can see it clearly, the rate of decomposition much faster than one can imagine. It has the foulest odor.

o. I have been wondering what would have happened otherwise, if one man, and then another, had not inserted themselves between us, if our pubescent state had not been hijacked.

p. Would our love still have died, inevitably, but without much notice of the fact, as if just one day I would look at my twin, my lover, standing in front of me, and I would have noticed that there was nothing more to say?

q. What would have been possible?

r. I'm commiserating to a friend about the disastrous and nebulous relationship between my sister and me, and how she's now, suddenly, found writing. I know it's a trick, a set up, a plot to stay always feverishly and desperately bound, like the person you trust most in the world, inch by inch, closing your throat, until you find yourself strangling to death. Borderline personality disorder means nothing to my friend. I'm trying to explain to him that this is not at all a good thing. He responds by telling me that I'm the only twin he knows who has such a difficult time with it.

s. I ask him the following question: *Do you know any identical twins that are women?*

t. He pauses, he stares at the air above him, charting all the pairs of identical faces he sees on a regular basis. *No,* he says, *I don't.*

u. *Desire pushes for recognition. It is less a question that we desire as much as it is that we be recognized.*—Lacan

v. If man's desire is desire of the Other, and if desire pushes to be recognized, then what does that make of us, Emma?

w. Do I desire women so that I may be closer to you?

x. Or do I desire women to be closer to the self? (i.e. Lacan and the Mirror Stage)

y. Dear Emma, I did a Google search this week. I typed in the search box: *Lacan + desire of the other + identical twins*.

z. I found an offensive number of studies reporting the link between identical twins and homosexuality, but no psychoanalytic findings on the irreconcilable space between identical twins and the Other, the self, and the object of desire.

Appendix:

i. I fell for Sarah Whitaker in sixth grade. I think. It's hard to recall. We went to the *King & I* as a class and shortly after, I snuck over to her house, alone, and I did fan dances for her while she watched me from her bed, lying on her stomach. You never knew about this, I don't think.

ii. I fell for Lori Poling in ninth grade. We spent the night at each other's houses, performed hypnoses and sang pop songs to each other with identical mud masks sweating off our cheeks. When she spent the night at Mom's house, we giggled in beanbags on the living room floor. You had already become everything that Gene wanted. You could seduce any man to offer you his disemboweled heart, moments before your rejection.

iii. You never forgave me. It was as though the rosebuds I swallowed suddenly turned to leeches tearing the pulp from my mouth.

iv. After Lori, I buried my heartbreak for girls. Our initial heartbreak was there, in an unnamed plot. And I died many, many deaths loving men. For a time.

DE PROFUNDIS by Oscar Wilde

Amanda Stern

The Marquis of Queensbury, who settles fights by fists and guns, has a dandy for a son. This frail and pretty popinjay, despised by his parents for his flamboyant ways, attracts the attention of a prominent literary figure, fifteen years his senior (who—to cover his own homosexuality—has married; with children). The two become inseparable, driving the dandy's illiberal dad to break them apart no matter the cost. It's 1895 and we're in Britain. Any sexual activity between members of the same sex is punishable by law—two years hard labor (where labor is literal) being the maximum sentence.

So begins the love story between Oscar Wilde and Lord Alfred Douglas (or Bosie, as he was known). The content, context, and costs of that relationship are outlined in *De Profundis*—an extraordinary letter, written by Oscar Wilde to Bosie from prison. How he wrote the letter, and all that led up to its production is as interesting as the letter itself. Allowed only one sheet of folio paper at a time, Wilde filled a total of eighty blue prison pages. You need not know anything of what led up to this letter—Wilde is fairly detailed on what occurred (and I break it down below); I didn't know the first go-round, but I do now and it's made the experience of re-reading the letter richer.

Bosie and his father despised each other. They wrote despicable letters to one another, hideous and abusive telegrams. Unable to tear his son from the man he feared was corrupting him, the Marquis of Queensbury went around town threatening to destroy any social establishment that allowed these two to share company. When finally he left a note for Wilde accusing him of being a "Somdomite" (sic), Bosie fanned the flames by mentioning, in a letter to his father, that *if* Wilde so chose to sue for libel over this claim of criminal behavior, he—the Marquis—would certainly find himself imprisoned for defamation of character.

Bluff called.

Against the protestations of his friends not to sue for libel—since, after all, it was not a false claim—Wilde, egged on by Bosie, told them they weren't "being friendly," and seeing this lawsuit as a way to verbally slay the Marquis, he let his hubris get the best of him, and with great eagerness, filed his complaint.

Oh, Oscar.

Resting his laurels upon his bon mots to win the case, Wilde, from the witness stand, played the prosecutor like a party-guest, lying about his age and then, flinging his witticisms around like a dust fluffer, bon motted his way into incriminating himself. Other plot-heavy things occurred, but what's most important to know is that Wilde was the instrument of his own undoing and was ultimately imprisoned for acting on his sexual urges.

I have read this book twice. Once, five years ago, and again recently. When I first read it, I was going through a break-up, and I lived vicariously through Wilde's anger and passionate scolding. *Yeah, Oscar! Give it to him!* I related to the book as the one who was wronged, accountable for nothing. *He should suffer for what he did to me! He should rot in a prison!* I loved this book because I so related and felt the anguished pain that Wilde felt while writing this letter. But then, this last round, I responded to it completely differently. Instead of being angry at Bosie alongside Wilde, I was angry at Wilde for staying with Bosie, angry at the wildly obvious advantage Bosie took of Oscar. I was frustrated with Wilde for his inability to hold himself accountable for his own shortcomings. When I re-read *De Profundis* I read Wilde as a meek simp without backbone or self-respect.

What a difference five years makes.

Diagnostically speaking, Wilde was a classic codependent and enabler, and hugely narcissistic. He allowed Bosie's opportunistic behavior, his explosive outbursts, abusive tirades and glutinous consumption on Wilde's dime, and in the end, he blamed Bosie for victimizing him—the tragic protagonist.

Bosie deserved plenty of blame, but Wilde's growth in prison—plentiful in many spots—is remarkably short sighted when it comes to his own culpability. This letter activates in the reader a reaction of some sort, and it's that reaction that makes reading this book truly absorbing. You learn not only about Bosie and Wilde's intrapsychic make-up, but your own. It commands you to judge and take sides, to question yourself, to feel something, because every one of us has written a letter like this, in our head or on the page; no matter the specifics of the relationship, and despite its personal dynamics, we can all relate to feeling wronged.

There are so many riches in this letter beyond the content (which is wise, insightful, beautiful, shameful, contradictory, and short-sighted, among many things). Take the conditions upon which this book exists: the instructions—to his literary executor—to have this personal letter, addressed only to Bosie, copied so that "some day the truth will have to be known." Much like reality television, where the viewer watches someone who knows he is being watched and cannot help but move or talk or behave with the self-conscious movements and expressions of how he wishes to be perceived, this letter is written to a readership as much as it is to Bosie. Therefore it cannot be truly authentic, which calls into question Wilde's motives for writing it in the first place. What Wilde did or didn't realize about himself, what he knew in his heart versus what he exposed, probably didn't quite align, but his suffering is true.

As I read this letter again, alerted to my own growth by my changed reaction, I wondered what I wasn't seeing this time around. In five years, will I respond differently again? And if so, what am I overlooking now? And so it goes, and that's why this book is a challenge. It might force you to answer to yourself. ❧

Index

The following is a listing in alphabetical order by author's last name of works published in *Post Road*. An asterisk indicates subject rather than contributor.